NEVER TURN BACK

An Illustrated History of Caister Lifeboats

NEVER TURN BACK

An Illustrated History of Caister Lifeboats

Nicholas Leach

TEMPUS

First published 2001

PUBLISHED IN THE UNITED KINGDOM BY:

Tempus Publishing Ltd
The Mill, Brimscombe Port
Stroud, Gloucestershire GL5 2QG
www.tempus-publishing.com

PUBLISHED IN THE UNITED STATES OF AMERICA BY:

Arcadia Publishing Inc.
A division of Tempus Publishing Inc.
2 Cumberland Street
Charleston, SC 29401
(Tel: 1-888-313-2665)
www.arcadiapublishing.com

Tempus books are available in France and Germany
from the following addresses:

Tempus Publishing Group   Tempus Publishing Group
21 Avenue de la République   Gustav-Adolf-Straße 3
37300 Joué-lès-Tours   99084 Erfurt
FRANCE   GERMANY

British Library Cataloguing in Publication Data.
A catalogue record for this book is available from the British Library.

ISBN 0 7524 2146-8

Typesetting and origination by Tempus Publishing.
PRINTED AND BOUND IN GREAT BRITAIN.

Contents

Preface

A century ago, in November 1901, tragedy hit the Caister lifeboat station when the *Beauchamp* lifeboat capsized near the beach trapping her crew underneath. Nine of the crew of twelve were killed. This disaster, one of the most famous and tragic incidents in the history of not only the Caister lifeboat station but also the RNLI, has been immortalised in the annals of lifeboat history. At the subsequent inquiry into the disaster, former coxswain James Haylett was called as a witness. At the suggestion that the lifeboat was returning having failed to complete the rescue and the crew had given up in their rescue attempts, he replied, 'No they never give up. Coming back is against the rules.' His answer has been famously misquoted as "Caister men never turn back" and this emotive phrase, which captured the public imagination at the time, has since become synonymous with the lifeboatmen of Caister.

Caister is famous not only because of the disaster and the considerable amount of publicity received as a consequence, but also because of the large number of lives saved by the station's lifeboats during the nineteenth century when it saved hundreds of vessels using the busy east coast trade route. The Caister lifeboatmen became famous during the Victorian era, when they were renowned for their bravery and courage. Today the station has the unique status of being the only independent all-weather lifeboat station in the country.

This book begins with rescue work in the nineteenth century, when shipping along the East Coast consisted of mainly small coasting vessels. Caister's lifeboats performed many services to these vessels which became stranded all too easily on the sandbanks that lay just offshore. The difficulties and discomfort experienced by lifeboat crews during a rescue in bad weather during this era are hard to imagine today. When oars and sail were the only options for powering rescue craft, lifeboats could be at sea for many hours, battling though severe weather, waves swamping the open boats which offered little or no protection for either rescuers or rescued. Once the lifeboat was at sea, the only aids towards finding a vessel in trouble were flares, rockets and a knowledge of the area. Sometimes the lifeboatmen had to get directions from the crews manning the lightships that marked the sandbanks and channels off the East Anglian coast.

The services described throughout the book demonstrate the great strength, both mental and physical, of the nineteenth-century lifeboatmen. The men who manned the lifeboats allied that strength to stamina and courage in undertaking the dangerous task of rescue at sea. As will become clear, almost every service performed by the Caister lifeboats during this era was to a vessel aground on the sandbanks, the dangers of which cannot be underestimated.

This history has been organised chronologically, although various themes, notably the problems of manning and launching the lifeboats, have been separated from the general order of events. In addition, the organisation of the station and the *Beauchamp* disaster have chapters to themselves. The rescues that have been described are a mixture of the most notable and the most representative of the kind carried out by Caister's lifeboats. While relatively few rescues have been described in detail, Appendix 2 gives a complete listing of all services up to the end of 2000.

The memorial in Caister cemetery to the nine lifeboatmen who lost their lives in the Beauchamp *tragedy of November 1901. These photographs show the fine memorial, erected in 1903, after restoration in 2000, and detail from the inscription. (Nicholas Leach)*

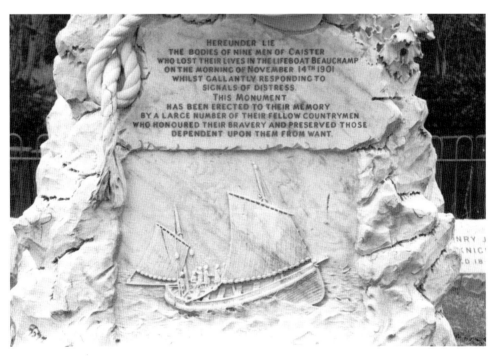

HEREUNDER LIE
THE BODIES OF NINE MEN OF CAISTER
WHO LOST THEIR LIVES IN THE LIFEBOAT BEAUCHAMP
ON THE MORNING OF NOVEMBER 14TH 1901
WHILST GALLANTLY RESPONDING TO
SIGNALS OF DISTRESS.
THIS MONUMENT
HAS BEEN ERECTED TO THEIR MEMORY
BY A LARGE NUMBER OF THEIR FELLOW COUNTRYMEN
WHO HONOURED THEIR BRAVERY AND PRESERVED THOSE
DEPENDENT UPON THEM FROM WANT.

Acknowledgements

During the preparation of this book, I have received considerable assistance from many people. In particular, information provided by Ivor Steadman about all aspects of the station, past and present, proved crucial and without his efforts to research and discover details missing from other accounts this book could not have been completed. Jeff Morris and Paul Durrant were also of great help in filling various gaps in the text. For supplying photographs for possible inclusion I am most grateful to the following: Paul Russell, Hitchin; Jeff Morris, Coventry; Paul Durrant, Caister; David Gooch, Dunstable; David Higgins, King's Lynn; Graham Brailey, Ivybridge; Roger Wiltshire, Norwich; Peter Edey, Brightlingsea; Gary Markham, Caister; and Eastern Counties Newspapers, Norwich. David Gooch and David Higgins, in particular, provided a series of interesting and unusual illustrations. Edward Wake-Walker and the staff of the Public Relations Department at the Royal National Lifeboat Institution's headquarters in Poole provided the facilities for researching the early history of the station. Sally Barter, Technical Assistance (Norfolk Studies) of Norfolk Library and Information Service assisted with various illustrations. Finally, on a personal note, my thanks to Sarah for her continuing support and patience during my researches.

1
The Coast Around Caister

The coastline of East Anglia is dominated by sandy beaches and soft clay cliffs that offer little resistance to the North Sea, whose force is constantly changing the shape of the coastline. As the sea gradually reclaims land, anything that stands in its way is under threat. Some villages, such as Shipden, situated between Cromer and the sea during the Middle Ages, have even been swallowed by the sea. The process of longshore drift has affected East Anglia to a great extent as sand and other material move along the coast, causing the mouths of rivers, such as the Yare, to silt up and beaches to disappear.

Offshore, the area is characterised by a series of sand ridges running parallel to the coast. In between these are relatively deep channels that offer safe passage for shipping. These shipping channels are artificially marked today, but centuries ago the sandbanks hidden beneath the sea presented a serious danger to the unwary mariner. Immediately off the coast at Great Yarmouth and Caister lie the Scroby and Cross Sands, while further north are the notorious banks of Haisborough Sand and Hammond Knoll. Further offshore, and to the

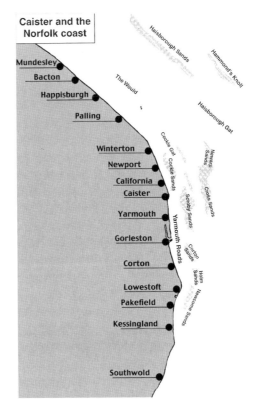

Map of the sandbanks of Caister.

south of Hammond Knoll, is the Cross Sand, a long bank divided into the North, Middle and South Cross Sands. Between and around these banks are navigable channels, but deviating from the channels proves fatal to most vessels. The ever-shifting nature of these sandbanks makes them notoriously difficult and hazardous to navigate as the channels move, alter shape, and change size as the vagaries of the North Sea currents take effect.

In this coastal environment lies the town of Caister-on-Sea, two miles to the north of Great Yarmouth, a small seaside resort with a pleasant sandy beach that affords good bathing. The town's name comes from the Latin 'castra', meaning a camp or fortress, and derives from the Roman era. A fort, the remains of which can still be seen at the western side of the town, was built here by the Romans who also used Caister as a harbour, but no remains of the port are visible. After the Romans left, the harbour silted up and a larger one to the south developed at what is now Great Yarmouth. As Great Yarmouth's natural harbour, formed by the river Yare, provided convenient shelter for ships, so Caister never developed as an important trading centre.

Hazards to Shipping

The development of the east coast trade route in the eighteenth and nineteenth centuries influenced the development of life-saving measures and the establishment of lifeboat stations along this coast. As the most direct line of communication between the important industrial centres in the north-east and London, the nation's thriving capital, the east coast was an extremely busy shipping lane. During the industrial expansion that took place between 1750 and 1850, trade was dominated by the movement of coal from the north-east ports of Newcastle and Sunderland to London. In 1779-84, forty per cent of coastal shipping was devoted to coal carriage. In fact, the coal trade was the largest single activity of coastal shipping for much of the nineteenth century. As well as coal, vessels carrying a variety of commodities crowded the North Sea shipping lanes making the channels along the Norfolk and Suffolk coast extremely busy. It was not an uncommon sight to see hundreds of vessels moored in Yarmouth Roads ready to enter port. An eyewitness account from 1838 stated that often as many as 3,000 ships could be seen at anchor in the Roads.

During the early years of the eighteenth century, the dangers of the seas off East Anglia were evident to Daniel Defoe when he commented that 'the sea-side on this coast, …is particularly famous for being one of the most dangerous and most fatal to the sailors in all England, I may say in all Britain; and the more so, because of the great number of ships which are continually going and coming this way, in their passage between London and all the northern coasts of Great Britain.' Unsurprisingly, wrecks were all too common. As early as 1692, a fleet of 200 light colliers was caught in storm off Winterton, to the north of Caister. Unable to turn for the safety of Yarmouth, 140 were driven ashore, smashed to pieces, and few of those on board survived. On New Year's Day 1779, forty-one vessels were wrecked on the sands near Yarmouth with great loss of life. During a storm on 30 October 1789, some eighty fishing boats were lost between Yarmouth and Cromer, and 120 bodies washed ashore. In February 1836, another storm claimed no fewer than twenty-three vessels which were stranded on Yarmouth beach alone, and these were just some of the many ships wrecked at this point of the coast.

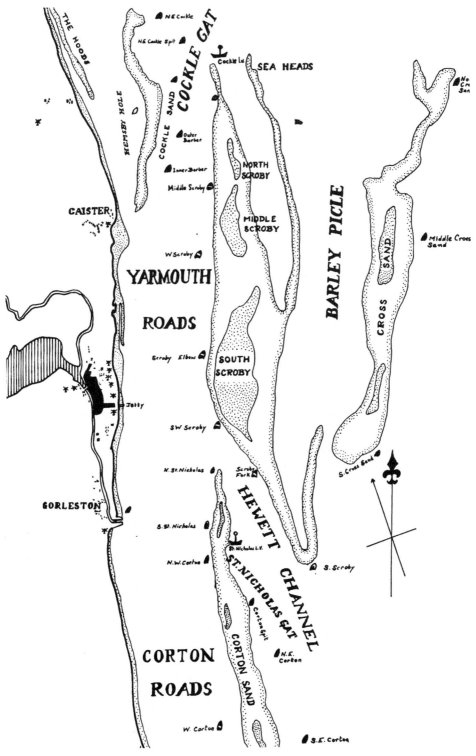

Map of the sands off Yarmouth about 1840.

The natural dangers of the East Anglian coast were bad enough, but small coasting vessels of the time were often themselves somewhat unseaworthy. Not only were they reliant upon and at the mercy of weather, wind and tide, but many were operated by inexperienced crews who found navigation difficult, a problem compounded by the inaccuracy of charts. Passing sandbanks was fraught with difficulties, particularly at night when the exact position of the hazards was unknown. The perils of the sandbanks off the East Anglian coast, combined with poor or non-existent navigation systems, badly maintained ships and winter storms, produced situations in which many boats were lost. Yet despite their dangers, the sandbanks off East Anglia had to be negotiated as they bounded an important trade route. Because shipping was the main form of transporting goods, shipowners and masters had no choice but to contend with shipwreck and the resultant loss of both crews and cargoes.

Early Safety Attempts

The first significant attempt at improving the safety of vessels off the East Coast was the introduction of lighthouses to mark dangers at various points on the coast. As early as 1600 the Brethren of Trinity House, the organisation responsible for the building and operation of lighthouses, carried out a survey of Yarmouth Roads which resulted in the erection of two lighthouses at Caister in 1628. A Mr Hill was instructed by the Trinity Brethren 'to exhibit in either lighthouse three candles of three to the pound which are to be lighted immediately after sunset and continue them burning until fair day.' Although there is no trace of these lighthouses today, they were certainly in existence when Daniel Defoe visited the town in 1722 for he remarked, 'that upon the shore beyond Yarmouth, there are no less than four lighthouses kept flaming every night, besides the lights at Castor [sic], north of the town, and at Gorleston S'. When the Caister lights were discontinued, the nearest major lighthouse to the village was to the north at Winterton, where a pair of lights had been erected to mark Winterton Ness and the northern entrance to Yarmouth Roads. The Winterton lighthouse was discontinued in 1921. As well as lighthouses on the shore, during the first half of the nineteenth century lightships were stationed at most of the dangerous sandbanks along the east coast between London and the Humber. 'Floating lights', as they were known, marked St Nicholas Gat off Great Yarmouth, the north-east end of the Shipwash Sand, and the northern entrance to Yarmouth Roads.

Despite the building of lighthouses and gradual improvements in navigation, vessels continued to be wrecked, and crews and cargoes continued to be lost. To overcome these problems, various remedies were proposed during the early years of the nineteenth century. One of the more practical was the use of a mortar to fire a line to a vessel in distress. As many ships were stranded close enough to the shore for a mortar line to reach them, such a scheme was viable. The main proponent of the mortar was Capt. George William Manby, who was born in 1765 and admitted as a student to the Royal Military Academy at Woolwich in 1777. After 1800 he wrote extensively on a wide range of subjects, including shipwreck. In February 1807 he witnessed the grounding and wreck of the gunboat *Snipe* at the mouth of Great Yarmouth harbour when sixty-seven were lost and only twenty survived. He was at this time the barrack master at Yarmouth, and after

A plaque from the monument erected by Capt. George Manby in his front garden, showing the use of his mortar. This is on display in Great Yarmouth Maritime Museum. (Nicholas Leach)

seeing this tragedy set about developing and improving the life-saving mortar using his knowledge of artillery.

After experimenting with various weights of shot, he finally adopted a $5\frac{1}{2}$in brass mortar which projected a 24lb shot carrying a $1\frac{1}{2}$in rope some 200yds, even against the wind. The mortar and wooden bed weighed 3cwt and could be carried on a specially built cart. The equipment was first used to effect a rescue on 12 February 1808 when the brig *Elizabeth*, of Plymouth, was stranded within 150 yards of Yarmouth beach. A gale was blowing, and the brig's crew of seven took to the rigging as their vessel was washed by the seas. Using his apparatus, Manby was able to fire a line to the brig, by which means all seven of the its crew were safely brought ashore. He was awarded the Gold Medal of the Society of Arts, the Silver Medal of the Suffolk Humane Society and publicly thanked by the merchants of Yarmouth for this rescue. In August 1810, Manby took his mortar to Cromer and demonstrated it on the beach. In November that year, it was used to save the crew of four from a vessel which had gone ashore at Trimingham.

As well as designing and operating mortars, Manby also travelled extensively around the country. In 1813, he published a *General Report on the Survey of the Eastern Coast of England* in which he noted the dangers of the seas and sands along the East coast, and made his own suggestions about what was needed to rescue stranded vessels off Caister. He stated: 'From the uncommon flatness of the shore, causing such high and lengthened surfs, must be attributed the number of lives that annually perished here.' He noted at Caister: 'From the nature of this shore, many circumstances of distress have occurred here, and as vessels are generally driven within 60 or 70 yards of the shore, a 6-pound mortar with stores, and a coil of $1\frac{1}{2}$-inch rope to haul a boat off by, will effectually remedy future calamities.' However, despite his recommendations, nothing was done at this time and no line-throwing guns were provided.

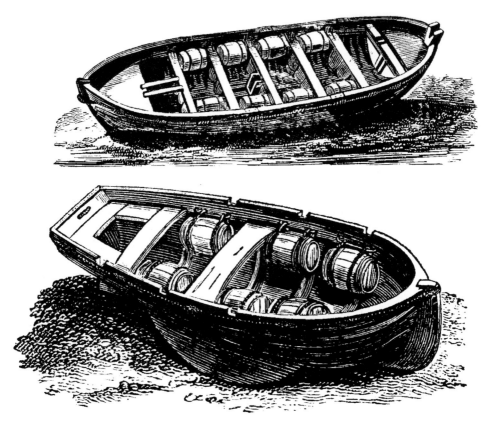

As well as his ground-breaking ideas for using a mortar for life-saving from wrecked ships, Capt. Manby also suggested that boats, such as the ferry boats used by the Yarmouth beachmen for landing fish on the beach, could be converted into lifeboats by lashing empty casts along the gunwales and under the thwarts, thus improving buoyancy. These illustrations show his how ideas could be put into practice. The man of war's jolly boat (top), described in Manby's 1812 Essay on Preservation of Shipwrecked Persons, has 'empty casks… well lashed and secured in it. For the advantage of keeping it in an upright position, launching from a flat shore, beaching, and to resist upsetting, it had billage boards of equal depth with the keel, and when a good sized piece of iron or lead was let into or made fast to the keel, if any accident did upset the boat, it immediately regained its original posture.'

The mortar was generally successful in helping to save lives from shipwreck and was adopted and used at various points along the East Anglian coast. After Manby's initial efforts, it was further developed by others, notably Dennett and Carte, inventors who used similar principles to those of Manby. By the 1840s, one was operational at Caister and it was used on 22 November 1840 to assist the vessel *St Rollux*, which had got into difficulty 130 yards from the beach. Two rockets were fired, but neither left the mortar due to various faults. However, a line was eventually got onto the casualty and all except one of the stranded vessel's crew were saved.

The Work of the Beachmen

The term 'beachmen' is given to the seafaring inhabitants of the coastal villages and hamlets of East Anglia who depended on the sea for their livelihood. The origin and organisation of the beachmen is a complex subject beyond the scope of this work, but the following is a brief background to their connections with life-saving, salvage and the lifeboat service, and in particular Caister lifeboat. They are well remembered as brave 'storm warriors' and heroes, but who also drove hard bargains when the fate of a ship was at stake and salvage money was to be earned.★

The beachmen were originally longshore fishermen who worked the North Sea, but later supplemented their income by attending to the needs of the ships that filled the sea lanes during the eighteenth and nineteenth centuries. As Great Yarmouth was the main trading centre, villages like Caister developed during the late eighteenth century and relied primarily on fishing. But by the 1790s, the Caister men became involved in other activities to supplement their income, notably assisting ships by taking out pilots to them, and salvaging vessels aground or stranded on the sandbanks. The salvagers were then entitled to claim a reward for their efforts, usually a percentage of the value of the cargo being carried by the stranded ship. As salvaging could be extremely lucrative, a thriving salvage industry grew up along the coasts of Norfolk and Suffolk. The men involved in this were organised into beach companies, and became known as 'beachmen'.

The vessels used by the beachmen were yawls, unusually large craft designed primarily for speed when sailing. The yawls were generally double-ended, had clinker-built hulls and were between 40ft and 70ft in length. Because they were expensive to construct, ownership was usually divided equally between the members of the beach company. Each member of a beach company bought a share in the company's vessels and gear, and took a share of the maintenance and repair expenses. The beachmen were usually governed by a set of printed rules which stated that no member of a company could share in the salvage unless he at least touches some part of the boat before she leaves the beach when launching to a vessel in difficulty. It was therefore a common sight to see men run into the sea to touch the extreme end of a yawl as it set out.

A salvage award could be quite sizeable in comparison to the relatively meagre income of the beachmen. In one instance in 1803, the Winterton beachmen were awarded a quarter of the value of the ship *Betsey* and her cargo after salvaging the ship. This amounted to almost £40 per man, a considerable amount of money considering their annual income was only about £25. The lucrative business of salvage was also a highly competitive one. In the race to be the first alongside a distressed vessel, and therefore claim the salvage, the beachmen's yawls were often involved in accidents, sometimes involving loss of life. The faster the yawl, the quicker the beachmen could reach a stranded vessel and claim salvage for their company ahead of rival companies. Caister beachmen were in competition with many others, including those from several different companies that operated at both Great Yarmouth and Gorleston, to the south.

Even if a vessel was assisted, the owners might contest the salvage rights and sometimes disagreements between beachmen and shipowners would go to court. For

★   For a full account of the work and lives of the beachmen of East Anglia see David Higgins, *The Beachmen*.

example, in March 1858 after the sloop *Margaret*, of Goole, had gone aground with her cargo valued at £230, the Gorleston beachmen claimed a proportion of the value of her cargo. The matter was settled in the Police court with solicitors and agents representing the owners against the salvagers. Claims and counter claims were made about the exact course of events. The owners claimed that although the sloop's anchors and sails had gone, no signals of distress had been hoisted and so the beachmen did not have a right to attempt to salvage her. Only when employed by the master could they claim the work of salvage had begun. The outcome in this instance was an award of £25 to the beachmen as salvers.

Not only did they assist to save ships, but the beachmen also saved those on board whose lives were in danger. In East Anglia, therefore, the first rescuers were the beachmen, albeit acting upon mercenary rather than altruistic motives. However, their salvage and rescue work was soon recognised and was regarded as so important that, in 1803, John Bickers and his crew of eight, all of whom were members of the Caister Beach Company, were exempted from impressment into naval service to fight in the Napoleonic wars. In their yawl, *Assistance*, the men were regarded as more useful 'assisting ships in distress, carrying off pilots and at the Yarmouth ferry' than serving in the navy.

The Caister Beachmen

At Caister, a Beach Company was formed in the 1790s by a small group of between ten and fifteen men who became involved in salvage work. Salvage and rescue work were carried out during the winter months, and fishing and other work done during the remainder of the year. The Company bought a new yawl in 1816, named *Prince Blucher*, and gradually increased in number. As many as eighteen men were registered as owners of the new yawl with equal shares in it. In the 1830s a number of other yawls were bought by Caister men and the company continued to gradually expand, rising to forty members at its height.

As with all the beach companies, the Caister men had a look-out on the beach from which they would keep a watch on the outlying sandbanks. As soon as a vessel was seen going aground, the yawl would be launched. The practice of manning the look-out continued even when the lifeboat became the primary means of reaching distressed vessels after the 1840s. The Beach Companies worked to a strict set of rules and regulations governing payments. Distribution of any salvage money the company gained was strictly limited, as was membership of the company.

The work of the beachmen was often dangerous and on occasions lives were lost, as in June 1847 when one of the company's yawls capsized. Perhaps the greatest tragedy to occur took place on 22 July 1885 when the yawl *Zephyr* was lost. She was launched during a calm night to a schooner seen stranded on the Lower Barber Sand for what appeared to be a routine service, with the moonlight to assist them reach the vessel. At the helm was James Haylett, Snr, one of the leading beachmen. As the yawl neared the sands, Haylett reminded the crew to look out for the mast of a sunkenstone-laden schooner, the crew of which had been saved by the Caister men in 1876. Just as they began to look, the port bow of the yawl struck the mast and the boat was torn open. Within two minutes, she had sunk leaving the crew struggling in the water. They managed to cut free much of the yawl's gear, and several

Caister beachmen in front of the company watch-house c.1870: Joseph Haylett, lost in the Zephyr *disaster in 1885, is on the boards outside the house and has the telescope to his eye; at the top of the steps is John Haylett; 'Matches' Hodds is next on the steps, close to Aaron King; the four at the front are, from left, William Knowles (also lost in* Zephyr*), William Read, John Vincent and Philip George; Robert Read is standing to the far right; to Read's right are Aaron Haylett and Isaiah Haylett. (William Read, courtesy of David Higgins)*

of the men clung to the oars and mast in an attempt to stay afloat. John George, one of the crew, set out for the shore and was picked up by a shrimper, *The Brothers,* of Great Yarmouth. The shrimper then searched for other survivors, and picked up six others including James Haylett, Snr. However, the remaining eight men in the yawl's crew were drowned, including James' son Frederick Haylett, leaving six widows and twenty-nine children father-less. The loss of eight men in the *Zephyr* was not only a tragedy for the families of those involved, but also for the village as a whole. The death of so many men in a village as small as Caister would have had a considerable economic impact on the local community.

The loss of the *Zephyr* came at a time when the beachmen's income was dwindling with little prospect of it improving. The beach companies throughout East Anglia were in general decline, due to a number of factors. Firstly, the start of trawling from Lowestoft in the early 1850s gave the men permanent employment in fishing, as trawling took place throughout the year, eradicating the times in the year when no income was earned from fishing. Secondly, income derived from salvage had greatly diminished as a result of the introduction of the railway company-owned steam-powered tugs which operated out of Lowestoft and Great Yarmouth. Their speed and power was much greater than that of the sailing yawls, they could reach and help stranded vessels faster, and so the beachmen's opportunities for salvaging

The grave in Caister Cemetery of James Joseph Haylett who lost his life when the yawl Zephyr *sunk, with a relief of the yawl on his headstone. (David Higgins)*

vessels in difficulty was inevitably reduced. The beachmen's reaction to the threat posed by the steam tugs was often violent and aggressive as they defended what they regarded as their natural rights to salvage. In October 1850, for example, the beachmen from Lowestoft threw stones from their yawl's ballast bags at the tug *Lowestoft* when the tug went to the assistance of the Aberdeen brig *Luna*. The tugmen had offered to get the vessel off the Newcome Sands for only £50, about one sixth of the sum expected by the beachmen.

The beachmen's feelings towards the steam tugs continued to run high during the 1860s and 1870s. The tugs undertook much of the salvage work and one incident, in October 1864, typifies the problems faced by the beachmen. Following the stranding of the Liverpool steamship *Ontario* on the Haisborough Sands during her maiden voyage that month, steam tugs from Great Yarmouth were employed in an attempt to refloat her. In addition, fifty-five labourers were engaged to take off her cargo in order to lighten her. However, all attempts to refloat her failed. The Caister lifeboat, intended to save lives rather than pursue salvage claims and fully discussed below, launched on three consecutive days to assist in the salvage operations to save the steamship and take off her crew, but on each occasion the captain refused to leave and forbade his crew from so doing.

On 19 October, with the wind gaining in strength and a heavy sea on the Sands, the labourers were taken off by the Caister lifeboat and put on board a nearby steam tug. On 20 October, the Caister lifeboat went out for a third time to take off the crew but again the captain would not let them go. The lifeboat returned to her station, but later in the day the crew did abandon their vessel which subsequently became a total wreck. Controversy followed this incident because no help had been received from the Great Yarmouth beachmen who had refused to get involved. They believed that the steam tugs 'had taken the cream, and they might do the remaining portion of the work.'

Caister village, as depicted in a line-drawing from the 1880s, showing the lookout on the beach to the right of which is the beachmen's shed. The artist is C.J. Staniland

The antagonisms and bad feelings towards the steam tugs subsided during the remaining years of the century, particularly when beachmen no longer relied so heavily on salvage for their income. The introduction of the Norfolk & Suffolk sailing lifeboats during the latter half of the nineteenth century, to be fully discussed below, also helped. The lifeboats superseded the life-saving role of the beachmen's yawls, although they were not intended for salvage work. As the lifeboats were not used for salvage, they often worked in conjunction with the steam tugs to save vessels and in many of the accounts of rescues that follow the role played by the steam tugs was significant. The lifeboats were manned by the beachmen, whose seamanship and boathandling skills were needed to operate these large craft. Thus the beachmen remained actively involved in life-saving work well into the twentieth century.

The First Lifeboats in Norfolk

The first lifeboat in East Anglia was stationed at Lowestoft in February 1801, having been built by Henry Greathead at South Shields to a 'North Country' design. Developed on the north-east coast, it was not ideally suited to the conditions prevalent on East Anglia's coast and the boat was disliked by the beachmen who were to form the crew and who preferred their sailing yawls, described above. Unused at Lowestoft, this first lifeboat was moved to Gorleston in 1802, but was liked no better there as its 'form not suiting the steepness of the shore' made it unsuitable and in 1807 it was sold. Although this first lifeboat was something of a failure, subsequent efforts to provide lifeboats at other places by locally formed committees were more successful. In 1804, a lifeboat was provided for Cromer, funded through local subscriptions organised by a local committee. In 1806, a Humane Society was formed in Suffolk which, among other activities, financed local lifeboat societies, and in 1807 had a lifeboat built to a design similar to the yawls favoured by the beachmen. In 1810, the local committee at Cromer established another lifeboat at nearby Mundesley.

By the 1820s, the idea of an organised lifeboat service had developed as Lord Suffield, a leading member of the Cromer committee, realised the need for 'an association for preserving the lives of shipwrecked mariners on the whole line of the coast of Norfolk', funded independently of the beachmen but relying on the beachmen for men and operation. Through the efforts of Lord Suffield, the Norfolk Association for Saving the Lives of Shipwrecked Mariners came into being in November 1823. This organisation took over the stations at Cromer and Mundesley and, at a meeting in December 1823, the committee decided to station further lifeboats at Great Yarmouth, Winterton, Blakeney, Burnham Overy or Brancaster, and Hunstanton.

At about the same time, the idea of a national body responsible for the provision of lifeboats was being mooted and at a meeting in London on 4 March 1824 these ideas came to fruition with the founding of the Royal National Institution for the Preservation of Life from Shipwreck (RNIPLS). The main motivator behind the new organisation, Sir William Hillary of Douglas in the Isle of Man, believed that a body, responsible for the preservation of life from shipwreck on a nationwide basis, was needed. By this time many lifeboat stations had been established independently, but no co-ordination existed on a national basis. The management and funding of lifeboat stations was undertaken locally. Many of the lifeboats in use, built in the 1800s, had been poorly maintained, under-funded or neglected, so by the 1820s improvements were needed.

Initially, the National Institution was quite successful and the new organisation ordered the construction of several new lifeboats. As a way of quickly and cheaply increasing the num-ber of lifeboats available, George Palmer, the Institution's Deputy Chairman, produced a plan which could be applied to all boats so 'they be made secure, as Life Boats, at the shortest notice: recommended especially for Ships' Boats, Wherries and Pleasure Boats.' As well as having new lifeboats built, therefore, the Institution funded the conversion and adaptation of existing boats for life-saving purposes. The conversion, which usually involved adding air cases to increase the boat's buoyancy, could be applied to any boat and so designs favoured in specific localities could be adapted and used as lifeboats. In 1828 the first recorded attempt to place a lifeboat at Caister was mentioned in connection with the conversion programme then being under-taken by the RNIPLS. At a meeting of the RNIPLS central committee on 24 December that year, the London-based boatbuilder, Harton & Co., were paid £58 7s for converting four boats to the Palmer plan: two six-oared customs boats for Caister and Corton (in Suffolk), and two Coastguard boats for Cromer and Lowestoft. Each cost £14 11s 9d, but no further records exist to detail what became of them. It is doubtful whether they were ever used for life-saving.

The first lifeboat at Caister, a 42ft Norfolk & Suffolk type built in 1846 at Great Yarmouth, as depicted in a model at the Science Museum in London. (RNLI)

During the 1820s and 1830s, the number of lifeboat stations gradually increased nationwide, and lifeboats also became more commonplace in Norfolk and Suffolk. But why was no such craft placed at Caister? Although it is difficult to say for certain, the lack of a lifeboat was probably due to two main factors. Firstly, the beachmen, with their large sailing yawls, were capable enough of helping vessels in difficulty. Even if a lifeboat for Caister had been proposed during the first half of the nineteenth century, the beachmen's yawls were probably regarded as being more than capable of fulfilling the role of a lifeboat. Although a lifeboat at Caister, situated just to the north of the harbour entrance at Yarmouth, would have been ideally placed to assist vessels entering or leaving the region's only port, the beachmen already fulfilled the role of rescuers and, more significantly, salvagers. Secondly, the Lord of the Manor, on whose land the Beach Company sheds were located, did not advocate the operation of a lifeboat. Whereas in many other places the local landowner or mayor was often the prime mover in the establishment of a lifeboat station, no such efforts were made by the Caister landowners. Had a lifeboat been operated from Caister, the salvage monies which the Lord of the Manor could claim from the beachmen as part of the rent they owed him would almost certainly be reduced, and it was therefore not in his interests to see a lifeboat in service. So it was only in the 1840s that the Norfolk Association suggested a lifeboat for Caister, by when the Association was short of funds with little prospect of increasing its revenue as it had ceased making public appeals

However, a subscription was raised in 1841 to finance a lifeboat for Caister, but it was not until 1845 that a boat was actually obtained for the station, and then it was a only second-hand one, built originally for Bacton. When this boat was found to be too small, leaky and in poor repair, the Caister beachmen refused to man it as a result of which a new lifeboat was purpose-built for the station. This new boat, designed by William Teasdell and built at Great Yarmouth by Branford at a cost of £150, was 42ft in length and had sails made by Bradbeer. Launched on Wednesday 11 March 1846, she was put under the charge of the local beachmen, but was never formally named. At the same time as the new lifeboat arrived, a look-out was erected on the beach from where the beachmen could keep a constant watch in bad weather.

Although no complete record exists of the rescues performed at this time, the Norfolk Association lifeboat of 1846 saved lives on many occasions. The Northumberland Report, published in 1851, stated that the boat had saved eighteen lives. On 17 December 1852, she not only saved seven crew from the schooner *Paulina*, which had struck the Scroby Sand, but also helped to save the schooner's cargo. The vessel had timber on board worth £800, but despite being waterlogged and having no rudder, the lifeboatmen got her afloat and took her into Lowestoft harbour the following day. The importance of saving cargo as well as lives was noted in *The Lifeboat,* journal of the RNLI★, of October 1853, which observed, 'Not only is life preserved to the mariner and beachman… but the merchant, the shipowner, and with them the entire community, are also reaping a large share of the benefit from the assistance which boats… render to property of considerable value, …which, without their aid, would otherwise be abandoned to the elements and become annihilated.'

The local Beachmen who manned lifeboats at Caister throughout the nineteenth century had a thorough knowledge of the sandbanks, shoals and seas off the Norfolk coast. This knowledge helped them perform many fine rescues, such as that on 23 February 1853, to the sloop *Hannah*, of Gainsborough, which was bound for London. The sloop was seen from Scratby riding close outside the Scroby Sand having lost her mast. Because of the surf on the beach, the Scratby beachmen were unable to launch their largest yawl, of about 25 tons in weight, so they immediately went south to Caister to assist the Caister beachmen. The two companies succeeded in launching Caister's 42ft lifeboat with a crew of twenty on board. Once afloat, they approached the wreck, which by this time was flying a signal of distress.

The passage under sail involved crossing the Barber Sand, and the north part of the Scroby Sand, during which the boat was completely submerged at one point in the heavy seas that were encountered. However, she succeeded in reaching the casualty after 'shaking off… the fetters Father Neptune had thus attempted to shackle her with.' The lifeboat's larger foremast and foresail were rigged to begin a tow, and the sloop was slipped from its anchor. The lifeboat then towed the vessel into Great Yarmouth harbour, where both boats arrived at about 4p.m. No damage had been sustained by the lifeboat, and the stranded vessel saved, its freight and cargo said to be worth about £1,000.

It was reported in the July 1855 edition of *The Lifeboat* that:

> *On the morning of 30th January, at daylight, a vessel was observed on shore on the Barber Sand, two miles SE of Scratby. The wind was blowing strong from East by South, and there was a heavy sea on the coast. The Seaman's lifeboat at Scratby was immediately launched, and proceeded under sail to the wreck, which she reached in time to save one man, another being taken off by the Caister lifeboat, which had also come to their assistance. The remainder, 6 or 7 in number, were unfortunately drowned, notwithstanding the efforts of the two boats' crews to save them. These boats and their crews are said to have behaved extremely well, under very difficult and hazardous circumstances.*

★ In the early 1850s the RNIPLS was reorganised and reformed, and in 1854 was renamed the Royal National Lifeboat Institution, the RNLI.

2
The RNLI Takes Over

By the mid-1850s the Norfolk Association had become rather tardy in executing its duties. Many of its lifeboats had fallen into disrepair due to poor management and maintenance. Indeed, in 1857 the Caister lifeboat could not launch when needed because she had been partially dismantled. Some of her air cases had been removed so that a local boatbuilder could effect repairs, but as these had not been completed, the boat could not be used. Consequently, when the ship *Ontario* was wrecked in October 1857, twenty-three of the twenty-four on board were lost. Change was needed and so negotiations with the RNLI began. These resulted in the Association's lifeboats and stations, including that at Caister, being taken over by the national body with effect from 29 December 1857. The Association had founded and operated nine lifeboat stations in Norfolk: at Hunstanton, Wells, Blakeney, Cromer, Bacton, Palling, Winterton, Caister and Yarmouth. The condition of the lifeboats at these stations was rather poor, so the national body's first task was to provide new boats and inject new capital to revitalise life-saving provision on this coast.

During the second half of the nineteenth century, the RNLI was in a strong financial position. Indeed, its finances were more healthy than at any time in its history. The work of the Institution's lifeboats, and particularly the courage of the volunteer crews, had been brought into the public consciousness in a way unknown hitherto. Popular writers, such as Charles Dickens, helped highlight the heroism of lifeboatmen, dramatising events that captured the popular imagination. With greater public support, appeals for donations were successful in increasing the Institution's income. The RNLI was therefore in a position to build many new lifeboats and increase the number of lifeboat stations. Once it had control of Norfolk's lifeboat establishments, it set about determining where new boats were needed and at which stations improvements were most urgently required.

The number of lifeboat establishments in Norfolk increased during the 1850s and 1860s as the Institution took on its duties in the region with enthusiasm. After examining the Caister boat in 1858, the Institution's District Inspector found her to be in good order so retained her in service and under the RNLI's auspices she performed many fine services, a number of which are described below. The first took place on 18 December 1858. At about 8p.m. that day *Propheta*, a large Portuguese schooner bound from Leith to Lisbon with a cargo of coal, was stranded on the Middle Scroby Sand in a gale, about $2\frac{1}{2}$ miles from Caister beach. The lifeboat was prepared and, according to the local newspaper report, 'plenty of stout and ready hands were found to man it.' She was quickly launched with a crew of about twenty men and coxswain Robert George in charge, 'a man who has formed the crew of the same boat on no less than 14 occasions.'

Once afloat, the lifeboat crossed the Barber Sands and reached the schooner to find it full of water and almost a complete wreck. Both masts were still standing, however, and the crew had taken to the rigging. The lifeboat was anchored to windward and veered down towards the wreck. Despite the heavy seas that were running over the casualty, the lifeboat was brought alongside and succeeded in saving the schooner's entire crew of eleven. These survivors were exhausted by their ordeal and exposure to the cold and wind. Once the last man had been rescued, the lifeboat set a course for the shore. She crossed the Scroby and Barber Sands, and despite shipping heavy seas safely reached Caister at about 1a.m. on 19 December. She was driven up Caister beach and the rescued men were landed. Sadly, one of them collapsed and was never revived despite the efforts of the local vicar and the surgeon at the Lord Nelson Inn.

Both the lifeboat and its crew received considerable praise for this rescue. No boat other than the lifeboat could have carried out such a service, and even then the schooner had only been reached just in time. Another half an hour and the vessel and its crew would have been overcome by the seas. Of the lifeboat's crew, ten out of the twenty had been at sea fishing during the morning yet, the local newspaper reported, 'when the hour of need came they were there and ready, and waited for no inducement or reward to proceed on their errand of mercy'. Although the beachmen's motives had been questioned on previous occasions, in this instance their conduct was described as 'gallant in the extreme'.

Just over two years later, the lifeboat performed another notable rescue. On 6 January 1861, she was launched to the brig *Arethusa*, of Blyth, which had gone ashore on the Cross Sand, near Great Yarmouth, and sailed to the casualty, having to cross the Barber Sands in the process. On reaching the stranded brig, which was in very heavy broken seas on the Cross Sand, the lifeboat saved its crew of eight and landed them safely at Caister.

On 26 February 1862, the lifeboat was launched to the brig *Sisters*, of Whitby, which had been driven onto the South Barber Sands off Caister. Despite the heavy gale blowing from the east, the lifeboat was launched through heavy surf, a difficult process requiring considerable effort from more than 100 people who were called upon to help. After an hour, the lifeboat finally got away through the surf, with the lifeboatmen pulling on the hauling-off anchor laid just outside the surf line. She then proceeded to windward of the wreck and veered down towards it. The seas were breaking over the casualty and it took the lifeboatmen over an hour to get the crew of nine into the lifeboat. On several occasions the lifeboat was lifted by the seas and thrown against both casualty and sandbank, incurring considerable damage. But she survived and returned to shore with the shipwrecked men through a heavy surf on the beach. According to *The Lifeboat* of 1 July 1862, this was 'a splendid service, and may serve as a suitable illustration of the dangers that have to be encountered by the skill, courage, and endurance that are often required of the brave fellows who man our lifeboat fleet.'

In the early hours of 4 May 1862, another outstanding service was performed by the Caister lifeboat. The schooner *Trial*, of Poole, was seen by the beachmen's night watch to be in distress on the Barber Sands. The whole of the beach company was alerted, forty in total, twenty-two of whom succeeded in launching the lifeboat through large breakers and shipping heavy seas. Once alongside the casualty, the lifeboat experienced considerable difficulty in getting the schooner's crew of seven off. According to the lifeboat's coxswain, Robert George, 'We hauled the lifeboat up alongside to get the crew out of her, but the sea broke so heavily into the lifeboat, sea after sea, which followed in quick succession, washing her crew about in all directions, we could not hold her, for the sea drove her quite round under the vessel's bow.' In saving three of the crew, the lifeboat was damaged alongside the ship and her mizzen mast broken. The lifeboat was shipping water, and staying alongside the casualty was extremely difficult in the severe conditions. But the lifeboatmen eventually succeeded in getting alongside long enough for the remainder of the schooner's crew to jump to safety. The lifeboat landed the shipwrecked men at Caister beach at 3a.m. having survived in the most difficult of conditions.

On 16 October 1862, a long service began when the lifeboat was launched to the steamship *Ontario*, of Liverpool, which was stranded on the Haisborough Sands. The steamship's captain declined the services of the lifeboat, however, as steam tugs were in attendance, so the lifeboat returned to station. The following day the lifeboat was again launched to the steamship, and this time the lifeboatmen helped to pump water out of the steamship. By 19 October the weather had worsened, and the Caister lifeboat was employed in taking off fifty-five labourers, who had been engaged to get the steamship off the sand, and transferred them to a steam tug which was lying nearby. However, the captain still refused to leave the ship, so the lifeboat returned to her station. She went off once more the following day, her third launch to the same vessel, and stood by despite the captain's continued refusal to abandon his ship. After the lifeboat had returned to Caister, the captain and his crew were forced to abandon the steamship, as it could not be saved, and they were brought ashore by one of the steam tugs.

Less than a week after the *Ontario* stranding, the lifeboat's services were again required. She launched on 26 October to the brig *Richmond Packet*, of Middlesborough, which was fast on the Barber Sands with seas breaking over her. The beachmen had launched to the brig in their yawls, but had to return to launch the lifeboat, which was used to save the crew of six who were brought safely to shore.

By this time, a new lifeboat was under construction for the station as this lifeboat had been condemned as unfit. The last services performed by the 1846-built lifeboat all took place in October 1865. On 1 October 1865, the brig *Nautilus*, of South Shields, struck the Barber Sands in a strong easterly wind, with heavy seas, at about 9p.m. The lifeboat was launched after signals of distress had been seen, and succeeded in bringing the brig and her crew safely into Great Yarmouth harbour. The RNLI's Committee voted £25 to the lifeboatmen. Just four days later, on 4 October, the lifeboat was again launched, this time to the brig *Harlington*, of Sunderland, which was bound for Lowestoft, carrying a cargo of railway sleepers. The brig had grounded on the Scroby Sand so her crew of nine were taken off by the lifeboat. The following morning, the brig was assisted off the sands, water logged and without its rudder, and was towed to Lowestoft. The *Great Yarmouth Independent's* report of the *Nautilus* rescue stated that the lifeboat had contributed to saving 113 lives from different wrecks, but was nearly worn out and about to be replaced by a new one funded by the people of Birmingham.

The last service performed by the Norfolk Association-funded lifeboat took place on 9 October 1865. At about 7p.m. that day, two guns were fired from the Cockle Floating Light, indicating a vessel was in difficulty on the Sands. The strong wind was causing heavy surf on Caister beach, but the Beachmen launched the lifeboat immediately and headed for the Cockle Light. About half-a-mile to the north-west of it, the brig *Kathleen*, of Hartlepool, was found at anchor close to the breakers at the edge of the Cockle Sand. The brig had hit the Light as a result of which part of her bulwarks and rigging had been lost. Her three crew had jumped onto the Light. The lifeboat veered down to the brig, and six lifeboat crew got on board her. They slipped the brig's anchor and took her to the north end of Cockle Sand, where they anchored and waited until daylight. At daybreak, the lifeboat went to the floating light, took off the brig's three crew and brought them safely to Great Yarmouth. A steam tug later brought the brig, with its cargo of coal, to the port. In the last three services performed by this lifeboat, she had saved a total of twenty-four lives. Between 1858, when the RNLI took over, and 1865, this lifeboat is credited with saving 133 lives having been launched twenty-three times on service. She had been at Caister for eighteen years and had enjoyed a 'glorious career' according to *The Lifeboat* of January 1866.

Nineteenth Century Lifeboat Designs

Before describing the new lifeboat about to be placed at Caister, it is appropriate to discuss the background to lifeboat design in East Anglia at this time. The accepted lifeboat design during the nineteenth century was based upon the sailing yawl used by the beachmen, described above. However, after the RNLI had taken over the Norfolk Association's stations, the Institution's favoured design of lifeboat, the self-righting type, was introduced to the beachmen and in 1858 a 38ft self-righting lifeboat was built for the Great Yarmouth station. The self-righter (SR) was a relatively new design, having been developed during the early 1850s when the RNLI was seeking a new lifeboat type with which to equip its stations. It was primarily a rowing boat, usually about 34ft or 35ft in length and with a somewhat limited radius of action. The beam of about 8ft meant the length to beam ratio was greater than four to one, whereas on yawls this ratio was much less making them more stable through the water.

With the RNLI now in control of Norfolk's lifeboat stations, the self-righter seemed a logical choice for service there as it was used almost universally throughout the United Kingdom and Ireland. However, the beachmen of Norfolk and Suffolk, who were to make up the crew, took an almost instant dislike to it, arguing its narrow beam would cause it to be upset more easily. They greatly favoured their own sailing yawls which were longer, broader with a beam of about 12ft, more speedy and had a greater range, enabling them to reach the outlying sandbanks more easily.

In April 1859, various beach companies in Great Yarmouth expressed their views on the subject in the *Great Yarmouth Independent*. They believed 'it impossible to combine the self-righting principle with all the qualities requisite to make them perfectly safe and efficient.' The Palling Company of Beachmen stated: 'We shall never be induced to venture our lives in a boat of that description [a SR] for the purpose of rendering assistance to shipwrecked persons in gales of wind or heavy seas.'

Trials were held at the end of the month under the supervision of Capt. Ward, RN, the RNLI's Inspector, in an attempt to settle the dispute. The outcome was that the beachmen's choice of boat would be respected and the RNLI withdrew the self-righter. The beachmen's favoured lifeboat outstripped the self-righter through the roads, particularly when under sail. When the 1846-built lifeboat was replaced during the 1860s, the new lifeboat was not of the self-righting type.

James Pearce, Birmingham No.2

In order for a new lifeboat to be sent to the station, an approach to the RNLI had to be made. The Revd G.W. Steward sent a letter to the Institution's Committee of Management in August 1864 on behalf of the beachmen stating that, as the lifeboat built in 1846 had become unsafe, 'On account of her age and long service,' he hoped that a new lifeboat would be supplied by the Institution. The RNLI's Committee of Management agreed that a new boat was needed and, having received four tenders, accepted that from Mills & Blake of Great Yarmouth. The new lifeboat was of the Norfolk & Suffolk type, similar to the boat it replaced, 42ft in length, equipped with fourteen oars. On 25 October 1865 she was launched from her builder's yard and on the same day was dedicated at Great Yarmouth. She had been provided by the Birmingham Lifeboat Fund and a committee of donors from Birmingham attended the ceremony, which was presided over by Mr R. Steward, Mayor of Yarmouth. Named *James Pearce, Birmingham No.2* after one of the first promoters of the lifeboat fund in Birmingham, the formal christening of the boat was performed by Miss Steward, the mayor's daughter.

Almost all of the services performed by *James Pearce, Birmingham No.2* were to vessels which had become stranded on the sandbanks, and this section contains descriptions of a number of them. The first service performed by the new lifeboat took place on the same day as her naming ceremony. As she returned to her station after taking the guests, including representatives of the Birmingham Lifeboat Fund, for a trip down the river, the crew observed the schooner *Maria*, of Hull, in distress on the Scroby Sands, in a heavy swell and strong north-westerly wind. They quickly reached the vessel, and were able to bring her to safety, despite the strong wind and heavy seas. Her next service took place on 8 November 1865, when she was launched to the brig *Raven*, of London, after rockets had been fired

James Pearce, Birmingham No.2, the first lifeboat supplied by the RNLI after it took over the running of the station. She served from 1865 to 1878, and this photograph probably shows her at her builder's yard in Great Yarmouth. (RNLI)

from the Cockle Lightvessel to indicate a vessel in distress. The lifeboat launched just after 6p.m. and reached the brig to find her on the Cockle Sands with one anchor broken and the second just holding. The brig, in ballast bound for Seaham with a crew of nine on board, and the master's wife, was brought to the safety of Yarmouth Roads by the lifeboat.

The next service by *James Pearce, Birmingham No.2* took place during the evening of 8 November 1865. The lifeboat launched during squally weather after a vessel had been observed in difficulty near the Cockle Sands. On reaching the casualty, the brig *Raven*, of London, bound for Seaham from Yarmouth in ballast, the lifeboatmen found the brig had struck the Sand and been driven over it. One of her anchor chains had broken, but the second was holding and keeping her from the breakers on the sand. The lifeboat crew succeeded in reaching the brig, which had ten people on board, and escorted it clear of the Sands and safely into Yarmouth Roads by the morning of the following day.

Another rescue performed on the sands took place on 11 December 1865 when the brig *Lucy*, of Sunderland, laden with coal, went aground on the Barber Sands. The Caister beachmen launched one of their yawls and attempted without success to get the vessel clear of the sands. The brig's crew refused to leave their ship and so the beachmen returned to shore, having damaged their own boat and been unable to render any assistance. About two hours later, however, a signal of distress was seen hoisted on the brig, and so *James Pearce, Birmingham No.2* was launched. The lifeboat crew succeeded in saving six men from the brig, who, after being landed, were taken to the Sailor's Home in Great Yarmouth. The brig subsequently became a total wreck.

James Pearce, Birmingham No.2 performed many fine services throughout the 1860s and 1870s. She completed six services in 1866, including saving twelve men from the steamer *Corbon*, of Newcastle, on 7 April. The steamer had become waterlogged and was unmanageable when the lifeboat reached her. On 30 November she saved eight men from the schooner *Coronation*, of London, which had gone aground on the Inner Barber Sand. The water was so shallow that the lifeboat was unable to get very close and to save the stranded men, they had to be hauled through the water tied to a rope.

On 8 February 1867, a night time launch by *James Pearce, Birmingham No.2* resulted in, according to *The Lifeboat* of October 1867, a 'very gallant service'. The sloop *Telegraph*, of Sunderland, bound for London, was at anchor in Yarmouth Roads when her anchor cable parted. The crew's signals of distress were seen at about 2a.m., so the Caister men immediately launched the lifeboat. After some difficulty they succeeded in reaching the stranded vessel, and found the sea was breaking over her. The lifeboat men, after hailing the stranded crew, got near enough to throw a rope to them and then, anchoring the lifeboat, veered down towards the vessel. The three men on board the sloop were then able to jump into the lifeboat. During this rescue, the lifeboat was driven against the vessel's stern by the heavy seas and struck the sand several times. She returned to Caister safely despite sustaining some damage.

During 1867 a second lifeboat was sent to Caister (a No.2 lifeboat, as discussed below) and *James Pearce, Birmingham No.2* was designated the No.1 lifeboat. In her new guise she continued as before, assisting nine ships during 1868, most of which had stranded on the Barber Sands. During the night of 23 May 1868 she succeeded in saving the Swedish barque *Balder*, which had struck the north part of the Haisborough Sands. Two fishing luggers, two steam tugs and the Palling beachmen in their yawls had

Caister lifeboatmen on board James Pearce, Birmingham No.2 *about 1870. This photograph clearly shows the clinker construction of the hull in which the lower edge of each side plank overlaps the upper edge of the one below it. (Caister lifeboat shed, by courtesy of David Higgins)*

attempted but failed to free the barque. As a last resort, the Swedish Consul at Great Yarmouth requested the assistance of the Caister lifeboatmen. Using the No.1 lifeboat they succeeded in getting the barque afloat after about two hours, and, with the assistance of a steam tug, beached her beside the Britannia Pier at Yarmouth.

During January and February 1869, *James Pearce, Birmingham No.2* went to the aid of four vessels. According to *The Lifeboat*, 'with the promptitude and skill which invariably characterise the movements of the Caister beachmen', the lifeboat was launched to an unknown foreign ship on 3 January which was flying signals of distress during a heavy SSW gale. However, the ship's crew managed to work her off the sands themselves before the lifeboat arrived. As the lifeboat returned to her station, the brig *Elizabeth*, of Blyth, was seen on the south part of the Cross Sands flying signals of distress. The lifeboatmen succeeded in saving the brig's crew of eight 'from their imminent peril' as the brig had been swamped and was about to break up.

On 15 February 1869, *James Pearce, Birmingham No.2* went to the assistance of the barque *Eliza Caroline*, of London, bound from Sunderland to Carthegena with a cargo of guns, ammunition and coke. The barque had gone ashore on the West Scroby Sands and, with the aid of the Scratby lifeboat, the Caister lifeboat helped to keep her afloat by using the pumps. A week later, *James Pearce, Birmingham No.2* saved the crew of twenty from the ship *Hannah Patterson*, of Bergen, which had been driven onto Yarmouth Beach in a strong north-easterly wind.

Another fine rescue was performed by *James Pearce, Birmingham No.2* on 22 February 1871 after the barque *Jane Kilgour*, of London, went ashore on the Cross Sands. The beachmen in their yawls initially attempted to free the barque, but when they failed the lifeboat was launched. She arrived on the scene at about 5p.m. and for three hours stood by the barque, which gradually filled with water. Once the lifeboatmen realised the barque could not be saved, they assisted as the barque's crew of thirteen abandoned their vessel. The men were then taken on board the lifeboat, which was towed into Great Yarmouth by a steam tug. The vessel subsequently became a total wreck and her cargo of coal was lost.

On 14 November 1871, both the Caister lifeboats, as well as the Great Yarmouth No.1 lifeboat *Mark Lane*, were launched to the steamship *Benjamin Whitworth*, of Middlesborough, which had grounded on the Cross Sand. Caister's No.2 lifeboat, *The Boys*, was launched first to the stranded vessel, and stood by during the night in case the weather worsened. By 10p.m. the wind had increased to a heavy gale and the lifeboat was being driven away from the ship. The lifeboatmen therefore returned to their station and launched the No.1 lifeboat, *James Pearce, Birmingham No.2*. In this larger lifeboat they were able to stand by until the steamer floated off the Sands. The Great Yarmouth lifeboat was also launched but her services were not required.

During 1875, the Caister No.1 lifeboat *James Pearce, Birmingham No.2* performed a number of notable services. On 29 January 1875, she was launched to an Italian barque on the Cross Sand. She proceeded to the reported location of the casualty to find a large ship, the *Oriental* of North Shields, which had been seriously damaged in a collision with a steamer. The ship's bowsprit had been carried away and she was in considerable danger, but with the aid of a steam tug and some of the lifeboat's crew, who boarded her, she reached the safety of Harwich harbour.

At about 10.30p.m. on 20 October 1875, with a moderate gale and a very heavy sea, a man swam ashore about a mile north of Winterton lifeboat station, north of Caister. He was the solitary survivor of thirteen from the 400-ton barque *Young England*, of Middlesborough, bound for London with a cargo of iron and wood. The survivor, almost half-drowned from his efforts to get ashore, stated that when he and the other twelve men had got into the barque's boat, the rope holding the boat had parted before the remaining four could board it. They were, therefore, still on board and as the barque was breaking up, there was no time to lose. The man immediately set off for Caister 'knowing that no boat could get off except the Caister Lifeboat... and never stopped till he had reached Caister Lifeboat Station, 6 miles distant, by which time, as may be supposed, he was thoroughly exhausted', according to the official report of the service.

The Caister lifeboat men had been watching *Young England* during the early evening but did not consider her to be in immediate danger, and saw no distress signals flying. However, as soon as the survivor reached the station, at about 3.30a.m., *James Pearce, Birmingham No.2* was launched. After finding the casualty, 'in the midst of breakers with her bow and stern broken off, a complete wreck', the lifeboatmen managed to get alongside and save the four men who were still clinging to what was left of their vessel by hauling them through the water using lines thrown from the lifeboat.

The report of this tragic event stated that 'the shouts, cries, and tears of joy [of the four rescued men] on the arrival of the Lifeboat exceeded all that that crew had ever witnessed.' The lifeboat did not reach the shore until 8a.m. on 21 October when the four survivors were safely landed. Out of the barque's her crew of seventeen, twelve had been lost. The four men saved by the lifeboat owed their lives to 'the young man who so gallantly plodded on through the storm, with his intelligence... of the 4 men who on the crumbling wreck were counting the moments.' Such dramatic accounts brought to the public's attention the work of the lifeboat crews. They helped to create an image of lifeboatmen in general, and Caister's in particular, as brave and courageous. Although they undoubtedly were brave in the extreme and performed some remarkable feats, it is unlikely this is how they saw themselves.

On 3 November 1875, another notable service was performed by the Caister lifeboatmen. The schooner *Harmston* from Newcastle, bound for Tarragona in Spain with a cargo of coal, became stranded on the Cross Sand during heavy weather. A large sea washed almost everything off the deck, including the two boats, and the schooner heeled over so the crew took to the rigging. Despite their exposed position, with breaking surf threatening to wash them away, they survived the night. At daybreak the Caister boatmen, who were watching from the beach, saw the masts of the vessel and immediately launched the lifeboat *James Pearce, Birmingham No.2*. To reach the casualty it was necessary to cross the Barber and Scroby Sands over which heavy surf was breaking. They found the vessel submerged and the crew shouting desperately for help while clinging to the rigging.

The lifeboat was sailed to windward of the wreck, her sails were lowered and the anchor dropped. She was then veered down towards the wreck, a dangerous task but one which was completed successfully despite the tremendous sea running on the sand. It was impossible to board the vessel, however, so a line was thrown into the rigging. This enabled a stronger rope to be hauled from the lifeboat to the crew of the schooner, and one by one they were dragged through the surf to the lifeboat. When the entire crew had been saved, the anchor was weighed, and the lifeboat left the scene.

The crew of the sunken ship was totally exhausted by their exposure, but, as the *Lowestoft Journal* related, 'a few drops of Jamaican Rum always kept among the lifeboat stores gave them fresh heart, especially as every minute brought them nearer to the place of safety.' The *Journal* ended its report of the incident by saying 'there is no company of boatmen on the entire coast of Britain who can show such a return of work done in the face of the utmost peril to themselves. The service rendered by them... in saving the lives of the crew of *Harmston* is only an illustration of similar performed for years past by these men, whose boast it is that where life or property is at stake, they are always to the front'.

The first service performed by the Caister lifeboatmen which was formally recognised by the RNLI with the awarding of Gallantry medals took place on 19 November 1875 after the schooner *Wild Wave*, of Sunderland, had been wrecked on Caister beach. Soon after striking the beach the schooner's captain was swept overboard and drowned, and a young lad on the crew was hit by a windlass with such force that he was killed. In such a perilous position, being pounded by waves on the beach, it was clear to those who were watching that the vessel would not last long and the three men still in the rigging were in great danger of losing their lives. The lifeboat coxswain, Phillip George, and the Chief Boatman of HM Coastguard at Caister, S. Bishop, led a large number of Coastguards and beachmen in attempting to rescue the three men. They waded into the broken water. When the mast came down with the three crew members still clinging to it, they were plucked from the sea and taken ashore where they were revived. For this rescue, the Silver medal was awarded to Coxswain George and Chief Boatman Bishop. Extra rewards were also made to thirty-five coastguard men and beachmen for the part they played in the rescue. When Coxswain George retired on account of ill health, having served for twenty-five years and assisted in saving a large number of lives, he was awarded another Silver medal by the RNLI. During his service in the lifeboat, he had been involved in assisting nearly 150 casualties and helping to save almost 1,000 lives.

At 8p.m. on 19 March 1876, the No.2 lifeboat *Godsend* was launched to a vessel thought to be on the Barber Sands in the middle of a snowstorm. The vessel was not perceived to be in immediate danger, so the lifeboat returned to her station. However, when the lifeboat men were hauling the lifeboat up the beach, signals of distress were seen from the vessel. As the tide had turned, and it would have been impossible to beat to windward against gale and tide, a steam tug was requested. The tug arrived at 1a.m. on 20 March and towed the No.1 lifeboat *James Pearce, Birmingham No.2* to the wreck, which turned out to be the schooner *Killin*, of Greenock, bound from Thurso to Yarmouth. In the heavy seas running, the vessel had been driven into the middle of the Barber Sand. The lifeboat was anchored as close as possible to it but she could not approach near enough to effect a rescue so the steam tug was sent to get the No.2 lifeboat, *Godsend*. In the meantime, the men in the No.1 lifeboat took advantage of the rising tide and succeeded in veered down towards the wreck. Although the lifeboat was severely bumped across the Sands, she got close enough to the schooner to enable the lifeboatmen to haul the stranded crew of five to safety using a line and life-buoy. They had been lashed in the rigging for five hours.

On 28 March 1878 the Caister No.1 lifeboat saved crews from two vessels that had gone aground on the Sands. The first vessel, the barque *Theresa*, of North Shields, went aground on the Barber Sand at about 7.45p.m. The crew of eight, together with three of the master's children, were saved by the *James Pearce, Birmingham No.2* lifeboat. While this service was being undertaken, flares were seen from a vessel on the North Scroby Sands. The rescued crew were therefore transferred to the No.2 lifeboat *Godsend*, which was launched for that purpose, and then the No.1 lifeboat proceeded to the second vessel. The lifeboatmen found the brig *Wladiener*, of Libau, riding at anchor just off the Scroby Sand having previously stranded on it. The brig was full of water, lying on her starboard side, so the lifeboat was taken alongside. With some difficulty, the lifeboatmen succeeded in rescuing the brig's crew of eight, after which the brig sunk at her anchors.

The No.2 Station

Many lifeboat stations on the East Anglian coast operated two lifeboats, and some rescues in which Caister's No.2 lifeboat was involved have already been described above. Of the two lifeboats, one would be about 40ft or more in length and be intended primarily for offshore rescue work in heavy weather on the outlying sandbanks to which it could be sailed. The other, smaller lifeboat, generally of between 30ft and 35ft in length and of

The two lifeboats on the beach at Caister seen in the mid-1870s. The larger of the two, to the right, is the first Covent Garden, *originally* James Pearce, Birmingham No.2, *while the smaller boat to the left is* Godsend, *originally* The Boys, *which served as the No.2 lifeboat until 1892, the first No.2 lifeboat on station. (Caister lifeboat shed, courtesy of David Higgins)*

smaller proportions, would be employed mainly close to the shore or in shallow waters around the sandbanks for which the large lifeboat was unsuitable. The need for such a boat at Caister was highlighted by two instances when lives had nearly been lost because a smaller lifeboat, able to work in shallower water, would have been of use. The July 1868 edition of *The Lifeboat* reported that the beachmen had wanted 'a small surf boat for inshore work'. Following the beachmen's request, the Inspector recommended in March 1867 that such a lifeboat should be stationed at Caister. Furthermore, he suggested a 32ft boat would be most suitable. The new lifeboat, built by local boatbuilder James Beeching at Great Yarmouth, was named *The Boys* having been purchased with donations received from *Routledge's Magazine for Boys*. She arrived at her station in September 1867 and was publicly launched on 10 September after being named by Mrs Routledge, wife of the editor of *Routledge's Magazine for Boys*. During their time at the station the No.2 lifeboats proved their worth and were called upon as frequently as the No.1 lifeboats.

The first service by the new No.2 lifeboat took place on 25 November 1867. *The Boys* was launched to the Norwegian schooner *Assistant*, of Stavanger, which was stranded on the Barber Sands. She remained alongside the casualty and assisted in getting her off the sands. The services of *The Boys* were next required on 29 April 1868: she stood by the iron-screw steamship *Lady Flora*, of Hull, which was ashore in heavy breakers. During the attempts to reach the steamship, one of the lifeboatmen was seriously injured by one of the lifeboat's oars which was driven against him by a particularly violent sea. On 30 December 1869, *The Boys* saved nine from the brig *Delegate*, of London, and almost exactly a year later saved the crew of ten from the South Shields brig *Joseph and Thomas*.

The No.2 lifeboat *The Boys* had been built with a shallower depth than the No.1 lifeboat so that she could work more easily amongst the sandbanks off Caister. However, when attempting to help the brig *Ark*, of Hartlepool on 22 March 1872, even the shallow depth of her hull was not enough to enable her to get close to the vessel. The lifeboat was launched at 9.15p.m. to the brig which had gone aground on the Barber Sand. On reaching the casualty, there was insufficient water for the lifeboat to get close, so the lifeboatmen anchored their boat and waited for the tide to rise. After about six hours of standing by in snow and squalls, the lifeboat was taken alongside, took off the crew of six and returned to her station, by which time the lifeboatmen were thoroughly wet and cold. The following day, as the brig had not broken up on the sands, the Caister lifeboat took out the captain to the vessel and, with the help of the Scratby beachmen, took her into Great Yarmouth.

While the lifeboat was able to assist vessels on the sand by saving their crews, getting the casualty itself into harbour, usually that at Great Yarmouth, was rather more difficult. On many occasions, the assistance of a steam tug or a passing steamer was called upon. In helping two vessels caught in a gale on 10 December 1872, *The Boys* enlisted the assistance of steamers to help her carry out a rescue. She went to the aid of the brig *Pallion*, of Sunderland, which had been fouled by another vessel. The brig was not stranded and so, with the aid of a steamer, the lifeboat succeeded in getting the brig and her crew of eight safely into Lowestoft harbour. While she was escorting this brig into Lowestoft, signals of distress were seen from another vessel. The second casualty, another brig, *Lady Douglas* of London, had sprung a leak and had several feet of water in her hold. As the lifeboat was already nearby she quickly reached the brig, and with the help of a steamer succeeded in getting the brig and its crew of six safely into harbour.

On 27 January 1875, the brig *Pike*, of Shoreham, was wrecked on the North Scroby Sands in heavy seas. As soon as signals of distress were observed, *The Boys* was launched under the command of Coxswain Philip George. She soon reached the distressed vessel, which was found in difficulty amidst heavy breakers. With some difficulty, the lifeboatmen managed to haul the casualty's crew, one by one, into the lifeboat. The rescue was successfully accomplished, and the lifeboat returned to Caister with the seven rescued men at 6a.m.

About midnight on 11 March the same year, the schooner *Punch*, of Caernarvon, was wrecked on the Barber Sands while on a voyage from Newcastle to Dublin. These sands, partially uncovered at low water, were particularly treacherous. As the tide flows, they became quicksand and if caught on them, a ship had little chance of escape. The crew of the stranded schooner lit a fire on deck and *The Boys* was launched to their aid. The lifeboat soon reached the schooner, which was quickly disappearing in the sand, but the lifeboat could not reach her as there was not enough water. After three attempts to get close had failed, the lifeboat was anchored close to that part of the sandbank which remained above water. The coxswain, Philip George, then leapt overboard with a heaving line and life-belt, and was followed by the rest of the crew. They struggled across the sand, sinking almost up to their shoulders at times, until they reached the wrecked vessel and a line was secured. The schooner's crew were then hauled through the broken water and quicksand until eventually all six were on board the lifeboat. The most difficult task was saving the master, who had been struck by the tiller and had three fractured ribs. The rescued men were landed at 8a.m. by which time the wreck had disappeared into the sand.

While the lifeboatmen were saving the crew of the *Punch*, another vessel was seen dangerously close to the sands. Although the lifeboatmen had warned her away, at daybreak on 12 March fragments of a ship were seen floating around the sands. The lifeboat was again launched and the area in which the wreckage had been seen was searched. Only the board on which the name and port of the vessel were painted was found. She was probably broken up as she was sucked under by the quicksand, with all her hands lost.

Alterations and improvements to lifeboats were made from time to time. When, in 1875, the coxswain stated that the bow of the No.2 lifeboat was 'too sharp', and she would not rise into the seas, alterations were made to improve the boat. The work was undertaken by Beeching; who lengthened the lifeboat by 1ft to 33ft 7in, improved the bow and fitted an iron keel to improve her seakeeping. Following these alterations, this boat was renamed *Godsend* after being appropriated to the gift of Lady Bourchier, of Hampton Court Palace. It was not uncommon at this time for lifeboats already in service to be renamed. The No.1 lifeboat, *James Pearce, Birmingham No.2,* was also renamed during this era, as described below.

The first services performed by the newly named lifeboat took place in November 1875. On 16 November she was launched after distress flares had been seen on the Scroby Sand. On reaching the edge of the shoal, the lifeboatmen on board *Godsend* saw a fishing smack aground amidst breaking seas. The smack's crew was attempting to escape in a small boat from their vessel, but were glad to see the lifeboat which took them on board. Having saved the smack's six crew, the lifeboatmen then stood by until the tide had risen sufficiently for the lifeboat to be taken close enough to the smack to board it. Even though it was badly waterlogged and leaking, the lifeboatmen succeeded in bringing it into Great Yarmouth harbour at 1p.m. on 17 November. Four days later, *Godsend* was again launched and this time saved the crew of six from the Norwegian brig *Brodrenes Haab*, of Tonsberg.

On 4 November 1876, *Godsend* was launched to the aid of the fishing smack *Phoebe*, of Great Yarmouth, which had gone aground on the Cockle Sand. By the time the lifeboat reached the casualty, it was already under water and the crew of six had taken to the rigging. Although the sea was breaking heavily over the vessel, the lifeboatmen hauled the six fishermen through the water and to safety on board the lifeboat. On 23 December 1876, *Godsend* was launched after flares had been seen from a vessel aground on the Barber Sand. On arriving at the scene, the lifeboatmen found the barque *Ingleborough*, of Hull, which had gone ashore after her anchor had broken while she was lying in Yarmouth Roads. Her crew of thirteen were safely taken on board the lifeboat and brought ashore. The barque subsequently broke up in the heavy seas that were breaking on the sandbank.

During the last three decades of the nineteenth century, the No.2 lifeboat *Godsend* performed more rescues than the No.1 boat. In November 1878, she assisted to save three different vessels, rescues that were in fact typical of those she performed throughout her time at Caister. On 9 November, she was launched to the barque *Augia*, of Guernsey, which had been in collision with a sloop off Orfordness, to the south, and was seen in difficulty in the Cockle Gat. The lifeboat helped to get the barque into harbour, with the aid of a steamer. On 12 November, she went to the aid of two vessels stranded on the Barber Sands, the brigs *Craigs*, of Whitby, and *Lily*, of Guernsey. *Godsend* assisted both vessels into Great Yarmouth harbour with the aid of steam tugs.

Much of the rescue work performed by both Caister lifeboats involved standing by vessels which had stranded on the sandbanks and waiting for them to float off with the tide. Therefore, most rescues were routine and relatively unspectacular, although the endurance of the lifeboat crew was usually tested. Their knowledge of the sandbanks was also vital as they often had to launch at night, as on 28 January 1879. On this occasion, *Godsend* was launched at 4.30a.m. to go to the aid of the schooner *Hermann*, of Berwick, bound from Hull to London. She stood by the vessel, which was stuck on the Barber Sand, until 1p.m. The lifeboat took off the schooner's crew of six, although the master and mate remained on board the vessel, which subsequently floated off the sands on the next flood tide. Less than two weeks later, on 9 February, *Godsend* stood by the steamship *Matin*, of Dundee, during the early hours of the morning. The casualty, bound from Boulogne to the Tyne, was on the Scroby Sand and refloated on the tide.

At 1.20p.m. on 7 March 1882, a barque was seen ashore on the Scroby Sand, where a heavy sea was running, accompanied by a strong wind. *Godsend* was launched and found the barque *Canmore*, of Dundee, bound from Dunkirk to the Tyne in ballast. The wind had increased by the time the lifeboat arrived at the scene, but she stood by while night fell. The lifeboatmen were concerned that the barque would break up, and so called the No.1 lifeboat *Covent Garden* (see below), which was at once launched. Fortunately, however, with the aid of a steam tug, the vessel was pulled off the Sands and, accompanied by the lifeboat, taken into Yarmouth Roads. The barque had a crew of fifteen men, and a woman and child were also on board.

Godsend continued to help vessels on the Sands, and on 5 January 1885 stood by the dandy *Tyro*, of London, which was aground on the Barber Sand until it refloated. Many foreign vessels were also assisted and two weeks later *Godsend* was launched to the brig *Triton*, of Svelvig, bound from Memel to France. The brig was in a dangerous position near the Scroby Sands during a north-east gale and a heavy sea. With the help of the lifeboat and a steam tug, the vessel, with its crew of six, was taken safely into Yarmouth Roads.

Although sailing vessels most often went aground onto the sandbanks because of strong winds, they also grounded in fog, which could be a particular danger. In thick fog, accompanied by a heavy swell, the brig *Primrose*, of Folkestone, went aground on the Barber Sand on 8 January 1890. When the fog cleared at about 3p.m., the brig was spotted and a yawl was launched to her aid, but the master declined the yawl's services and requested the lifeboat instead. So at 5.30p.m. *Godsend* was launched and stood by the ship until she floated with the rising tide. Fog was again to blame when the Great Yarmouth fishing dandy *Florence Mary* was stranded on 16 June 1890 on the North Scroby Sand while returning from fishing. *Godsend* was launched and found the dandy, with a crew of six men. The lifeboat stood by until the tide rose and the vessel floated off the sand without the lifeboat's assistance.

The last services performed by *Godsend* took place in 1891, and were of a routine nature. On 8 December 1891 she stood by the West Hartlepool brig *Queen of the Isles*, and on 28 December saved the schooner *Hannah Ransom* and her crew of five. In January 1892, *Godsend* was replaced as the No.2 lifeboat and was subsequently sold by the RNLI. She had served the station for twenty-four years during which time she gained an impressive record of life-saving, launching 128 times on service and saving 410 lives.

The Covent Garden Lifeboats

In 1878, the lifeboat *James Pearce, Birmingham No.2* was renamed *Covent Garden* after being appropriated to the Covent Garden Lifeboat Fund. It was not uncommon for lifeboats in the nineteenth century to be renamed and appropriated to different donors. This lifeboat became the first of three to be provided by the Covent Garden Fund, one of many such funds set up by different groups during the late nineteenth century to raise funds for charitable purposes. As the No.1 lifeboat she continued to perform rescues mainly on the outlying sandbanks, sometimes assisting and sometimes being assisted by the No.2 lifeboat. The first service of the newly-named *Covent Garden* lifeboat took place on 6 November 1878 after flares had been seen in the direction of the Cross Sand. The lifeboatmen put out in *Covent Garden* and found the fishing smack *Mystery*, of Great Yarmouth, partly dismantled and abandoned by her crew. They boarded the smack and sailed her into Yarmouth Roads where she was anchored until the following morning. At daybreak a steam tug towed her into Yarmouth Harbour.

Rescue work for the Caister lifeboats was not always easy, and although the lifeboat crew demonstrated great stamina and skill in effecting rescues, the work sometimes damaged their lifeboat as happened on 28 December 1879. At 4p.m. flares were seen from the direction of the Cross Sand and so *Covent Garden* was launched into heavy seas. She reached the Cross Sand, where the brig *Rival*, of Blyth, was found in the middle of a breach of the sea on Middle Cross Sand. The lifeboatmen succeeded in getting the boat anchor off the Sand and saved the crew of eight. The seas were breaking over the casualty as high as the fore top. In these conditions the lifeboat suffered some damage when her rudder was lost, but once she returned to station, repairs were effected by local boatbuilder Beeching.

During November 1880, *Covent Garden* performed three services in quick succession. At about 3a.m. on the 1st she launched to the fishing smack *Iron Duke*, of London, which was drifting without her anchor near the Cross Sand. The lifeboat crew boarded her and, with the aid of a steam tug, took her and her crew of six safely into Yarmouth harbour. On the 6th *Covent Garden* put off to the steamship *Swan*, which had struck the Haisborough Sands, but steam tugs assisted the vessel to safety. Finally, on the 16th she was launched at 5a.m. after signals of distress seen on the Middle Scroby Sand. The lifeboatmen found the steamship *Ringdove*, of Liverpool, ashore on the sands. With great difficulty, and at considerable risk to the lifeboat, some of the shipwrecked men were hauled to safety by means of lines thrown to them. Others were able to jump into the lifeboat's stern which was brought near to the

The second of the Covent Garden *lifeboats to serve at Caister. This photograph was probably taken at Great Yarmouth on 3 November 1883, the day of the boat's naming ceremony. Together with the lifeboatmen, on board the lifeboat are various members of the Committee of the Covent Garden Lifeboat Fund. (RNLI)*

stranded vessel, and in all sixteen men were saved. Heavy seas were breaking over both lifeboat and ship throughout the difficult rescue.

The last service performed by the first *Covent Garden* lifeboat took place on 20 October 1883. She was launched at about 3a.m. after guns and rockets had been fired by the Cockle and St Nicholas lightships, indicating a vessel in trouble on the sands. On reaching the area, the lifeboat found the barque *Arab*, in ballast from London to Newcastle with a crew of fifteen, in the centre of the Middle Cross Sand. The lifeboat anchored and veered down towards the barque enabling the lifeboatmen to board her, albeit with some difficulty. They managed to get the vessel off the sand and then engaged a steam tug to tow her into Great Yarmouth.

Originally *James Pearce, Birmingham No.2*, the *Covent Garden* lifeboat was the first at Caister provided by the RNLI. By the 1880s, she had served the station for almost two decades, during which many notable services had been performed and 484 lives saved. Several months before the service to *Arab*, it had been reported to the RNLI's Committee of Management that she was unfit for service. As the coxswain and crew were unwilling to use the boat, the Institution decided a new one should be built for the station. In August 1883, Beeching's tender of £320 to build a new 42ft fourteen-oared lifeboat was accepted. By the end of October the new lifeboat was ready and on 1 November it was sent to Caister.

As explained in *The Lifeboat* of August 1884, the new lifeboat was again named *Covent Garden* 'in acknowledgement of the handsome collection made each year on behalf of the Institution through the co-operation of the Stewards of the special lifeboat Fund promoted amongst the trades people and others connected with Covent Garden Market.' The formal naming of the new lifeboat took place at Great Yarmouth, on 3 November 1883, in the presence of H.R. Buck, C. Denton, A. Dickson, S.J. Pallant and J. Webber, members of the Committee of the Covent Garden Lifeboat Fund, who had travelled from London in order to attend. A service of dedication was conducted by the Revd E.G.H. Murrell, honorary secretary of the Caister Branch, after which the Mayoress of Yarmouth named the lifeboat, 'and the new craft glided into the water in gallant style amid the cheers of the spectators,' as *The Lifeboat* grandiosely described events. In fine weather, a steam tug towed the new lifeboat round to the Britannia Pier and then back to her station.

The first service performed by the second *Covent Garden* took place on 18 November 1883, less than a month after she had been placed on station. She launched at 1a.m. after flares had been seen in the direction of the North Scroby Sand. She reached the area to find the barge *Garson,* of Wisbech, riding at anchor and apparently about to sink. The barge's crew of four were taken on board the lifeboat, which then stood by the casualty for some time. When the wind and sea became so strong that standing by became too dangerous, the lifeboat was sailed to Great Yarmouth where the four men from the barge were landed.

In March 1885 two fine services were performed on successive days. At 9p.m. on 8 March *Covent Garden* was launched after flares had been seen in the vicinity of the Cross Sand. On reaching the Sand the lifeboatmen found the three-masted schooner *Akyab*, of Genoa, bound for Hull from Cyprus. With the lifeboat's assistance, and that of a yawl and steam tug, the vessel was got afloat and then made for Harwich. The lifeboat escorted her southwards throughout the night.

On nearing the Shipwash Lightship, off the Suffolk coast and some distance from her station, the lifeboatmen saw the steamship *Beale*, of Scarborough, on the Shipwash Sand flying signals of distress at about 7a.m. the following day. The lifeboat immediately sailed to her aid, tried to get her afloat, and stood by as the weather was deteriorating. The steamer was bound for the south of France with a cargo of coal-tar pitch. The crew of a yawl, which had arrived to help, were then employed in throwing the cargo overboard to lighten her in an attempt to free her. After working for some time, the weather got so bad that the yawl's crew were forced to abandon the ship. The wind continued to increase and as seas were breaking right over the vessel, her crew of

Another illustration by C.J. Staniland vividly shows the second Covent Garden *being launched. Although Staniland uses artistic licence to increase the drama of the scene, the difficulty of launching from an open beach is clear. The lifeboatmen in the boat are probably pulling on a haul-off warp to get clear of the beach. The haul-off warp was a rope laid off the beach which the crew used to get the lifeboat through the surf and away.*

nineteen men, a pilot and a dog were taken on board the lifeboat and landed at Harwich at about 5p.m.

The lifeboat remained in Harwich overnight and at about 7a.m. the following day, 10 March, set out again for the steamship in the tow of a steam tug. The casualty had not taken on much water during the night and the yawl's crew again boarded her. A steam tug brought the casualty's crew out to her, and in a combined effort the vessel was floated off the sands. She was towed to Harwich, reaching the harbour at about 11p.m., where *Covent Garden* stayed for a second night. Having been operating well out of her usual area of service, she set out at 6a.m. the following morning, and reached Caister at 1p.m. after a long service that tested the crew's stamina and levels of endurance.

The sandbanks off Caister proved to be major hazards to vessels travelling down the East coast and many East Anglian lifeboat services were to vessels caught out by the ever-shifting banks. A long service to a vessel on the sands was undertaken by *Covent Garden* in 1888. At 8.30a.m. on 15 March that year *Covent Garden* was launched after the Middle Cross Sand Lightship fired guns indicating a vessel was on the Sands. The large full-rigged ship *Andromeda*, of Geestemunde, bound for New York from Bremen in ballast, was aground. Her mast had gone and two small boats were hanging from the jib boom end with thirteen men in them. A rope was got to the boats with difficulty and they were

Almost all of the rescues performed by the Caister lifeboat in the nineteenth century involved it going to one of the many sandbanks on which vessels were always becoming stranded. To reach a stranded vessel and save the lives of those on board, the lifeboat often had to be anchored close to the sandbank as there was insufficient depth of water in which the lifeboat could operate. Once anchored, the lifeboatmen would then wade through the shallow water across the sand to reach the casualty. C.J. Staniland depicts in dramatic fashion such a rescue with the lifeboatmen approaching the wreck ready to save a lone survivor lashed to the mast.

towed clear of the surf. Some of the occupants were taken on board the lifeboat, and some of the lifeboat's crew were put onto the boats to look after them.

After this, further attempts were made to get the three other men off the ship but without success. A tug arrived but could not help as seas were continually breaking over both the casualty and the lifeboat. As nothing could be done, the lifeboat anchored and the tug took the rescued crews to Yarmouth. As night approached, with the tide falling, another approach was made. With the help of the tug, the lifeboat got into a position whereby she could reach the ship. Once alongside, each man waited on the word from the coxswain before coming down into the lifeboat. The heavy seas washing over the boat the whole time meant that the lifeboat crew had to use great skill and effort to effect a successful rescue.

Once the three men had been saved, the lifeboat left the scene and was towed to Yarmouth harbour where the survivors were landed. The Master's face was badly cut and

One of a series of nineteenth century illustrations by the artist C.J. Staniland depicting lifeboat work of the time. As he lived at Caister during the 1870s, most of his drawings show the station's lifeboat, the second Covent Garden. *This dramatic illustration shows the lifeboat being prepared for launching, with the lifeboat men rushing to her and the blocks being removed.*

others with injuries were taken to Yarmouth Hospital. The lifeboat crew stayed in Yarmouth, as they were thoroughly drenched and hungry. Having launched at 8.30a.m., and having reached the vessel an hour later, it was not until 5.30p.m. that the lifeboat arrived in Yarmouth, and not until the following morning that she returned to Caister. A special reward from the Institution was presented to Coxswain James Haylett and the lifeboat's twenty crew for this rescue.

In many instances, the lifeboat was assisted by one of the beachmen's yawls in helping vessels in distress, particularly in cases where the weather was moderate. This was the case on 14 May 1891, when the watchman on Caister beach saw the flash of a gun north of the Cross Sand at about 3a.m. A yawl was launched in moderate seas, and *Covent Garden* also launched to help. On reaching the area, the steamship *Cambria*, of Dundee, bound for London, was found badly damaged after it had collided with a steam collier on the North shoal of the Cross Sand. The steamship's passengers were taken to the lightvessel in the steamer's boats for safety. The lifeboat stood by the damaged steamer while the yawl took the passengers off the lightvessel. The yawl then sailed to Great Yarmouth with seventeen persons from the steamer, while the lifeboatmen stayed with the casualty and made every effort to save her. However, the weather worsened throughout the day, and by the early hours of 15 May the master and the remainder of the crew abandoned ship, took to their boat, which was hauled to the lifeboat, and then were taken by the lifeboat to Great Yarmouth.

On many occasions the No.1 and No.2 lifeboats would work together to save a vessel and its crew. On 9 February 1894 with a strong WSW gale blowing, the 1,032-ton steamship *Resolven*, of Cardiff, bound from North Shields for Lisbon with coal, was stranded on the Barber Sand. The No.2 lifeboat *Beauchamp* was launched and, as eighty-one labourers and a crew of twenty-one were on board, the No.1 lifeboat *Covent Garden* was also launched. About 150 tons of coal was thrown overboard, and three tugs tried, without success, to tow the vessel off. During the morning of 10 February the steamship's engines broke down and the engine room filled with water. By midnight the ship was almost full of water. At 11a.m. the following morning, with the sea was breaking over her, she was clearly breaking up. *Beauchamp* took off thirty-five of the labourers and *Covent Garden* took off forty-six, all of whom were put on board a steam tug. *Beauchamp* returned to Caister while *Covent Garden* stood by the wreck to rescue the master and crew. They waited until any possibility of saving the ship had gone and, when the seas began to sweep over her, got into the lifeboat which landed them at Great Yarmouth.

The last service performed by the second *Covent Garden* lifeboat took place on 23 February 1896. After the Cockle lightvessel had fired rockets indicating she was needed, the lifeboat was readied for launching. While she was being launched a coastguard man arrived and informed the coxswain that a barque was aground on the south-east Haisborough Sand. The lifeboat sailed through heavy seas to reach the Sands, but as the lifeboat men found nothing, they proceeded along the sand until they found the barque *Glenbervie*, of Glasgow, with a crew of eighteen men, bound for Adelaide. The lifeboat went alongside and, after discussions with the master, agreed to help guide the barque to safety. With the assistance of two steam tugs which subsequently arrived, she was taken to Harwich through the strong gale and heavy seas. The lifeboat returned to Great Yarmouth the following evening, having sheltered in Harwich harbour.

By 1898, *Covent Garden* was beginning to show her age and was also regarded as somewhat out of date. Improvements to the Norfolk & Suffolk design had been developed following the lifeboat trials at Lowestoft of 1892. These trials had shown that water ballast tanks greatly improved the sea-keeping ability of the design, while drop keels improved performance under sail. In September the Honorary Secretary contacted the RNLI and stated that the beachmen wanted a new No.1 lifeboat 'fitted with all the latest improvements'. The Committee of Management approved this request, and ordered from the Thames Iron Works in Blackwall, London, a new Norfolk & Suffolk type, 40ft in length and 12ft in breadth, in accordance with the wishes of the crew. In December, £566 17s 6d was received from the Covent Garden Lifeboat Fund to pay for the new lifeboat. A year later, on 4 December 1899, the new lifeboat was satisfactorily put through her harbour trial, and the following day went to Caister to become the new No.1 lifeboat. This lifeboat, the third and last of the *Covent Garden* lifeboats, was built at a total cost of £1,295 7s 5d and, being of the 'improved' Norfolk & Suffolk type, was fitted with four water ballast tanks and two drop keels.

The new lifeboat did not perform her first effective service until she had been on station for more than a year. On 21 January 1901, after flares had been seen in the direction of the Scroby Elbow Sand during the morning, she was launched and found the schooner *Bertha*, of Great Yarmouth, just floating off the sands with the rising tide. The crew had deserted their vessel and were seen taking refuge on board the St Nicholas Lightvessel. With the assistance of steam tugs the schooner, which had lost her rudder and had water in her hold, was taken into Great Yarmouth harbour.

The system of alerting lifeboats to a vessel stranded on the sands off Norfolk's coast would only work if the vessel was seen by those manning the lightvessels. When the schooner *Jasper*, of Fowey, bound from Plymouth to Hull with a cargo of china clay,

A very good view of the third Covent Garden *lifeboat on the beach. The large cork belt around the gunwale and clinker-built hull, typical of the large Norfolk & Suffolk type lifeboats of the era, are clearly visible. (From an old postcard supplied by a Shoreline member)*

ran aground on the Haisborough Sands on 16 January 1904, she was not seen. Her crew were forced to abandon her, and using one of the ship's boats began to row for one of the lightvessels. However, heavy seas continually broke over the boat, drenching those on board. Constant baling was required to keep it afloat, but the exposure was so great that one of the crew died. After nine hours they succeeded in reaching the Newarp lightvessel, climbed on board and were tended by the light keepers, who also transferred the body of the dead man to the lightvessel. Early next morning, following signals fired from the lightvessel, *Covent Garden* was launched and took the ship-wrecked men on board. The lifeboat was towed to Great Yarmouth by a steam tug where the survivors were landed.

During the afternoon of 15 February 1907, the lifeboatmen were attending the funeral of former Coxswain James Haylett when the lifeboat bell was rung. As soon as they could, the crew hurried to the beach and launched *Covent Garden*. The brand new trawler *Francis Roberts*, of Lowestoft, had stranded on the Barber Sands with all her sails set. After the master had failed in his attempts to get the vessel off, the lifeboatmen assisted. After two hours, using an anchor laid out from the vessel, they succeeded in getting the vessel clear. The trawler was then taken to Lowestoft, one of the lifeboatmen accompanying her.

As well as both Caister lifeboats working together, they often worked with lifeboats from neighbouring stations to help a vessel. On 20 May 1907, when two torpedo-boat destroyers got into difficulty near the Barber Sand ran aground, both *Covent Garden* and the Great Yarmouth lifeboat *John Burch* were launched to help. *Covent Garden* went to the aid of HMS *Cherwell*, while *John Burch* went to HMS *Ettrick*. The two lifeboats 'rendered valuable assistance in getting the vessels off', a particularly valuable service as on board each ship were crews of seventy men.

Many services performed by the Caister lifeboat involved travelling considerable distances to the outlying sandbanks where the lifeboat would stand by vessels in difficulty. Often the situation of the casualty was not deteriorating sufficiently to warrant a rescue, so the lifeboat would stand by for hours until the danger to the vessel had passed. One such incident took place in November 1907 after the steamer *Terra,* of Glasgow, was stranded on the Cockle Sands, about twelve miles from the mainland close to Hemsby Gap, and south of the North East Cockle Buoy. The No.1 lifeboat *Covent Garden*, used for the more arduous services, was launched at 11p.m. on 22 November. Although no service was performed, as the casualty was eventually refloated after several thousand tons of coal had been removed from her, the lifeboat did not return to her station until noon the following day. During the salvage operation no fewer than six tugs were employed in hauling this steamer off the sands. Sixty labourers from Great Yarmouth also assisted with the operation after which the vessel was towed by tugs to a safe anchorage, with both Winterton and Caister lifeboats standing by her. On this occasion although their services were not needed, the rough seas made the work of those manning both tug and lifeboat very difficult. The Caister lifeboatmen, accompanied by the secretary of the Lifeboat Committee, Mr A. Clowes, were all thoroughly soaked by the time they returned to the station.

In the early morning of 21 September 1909, the Coastguard reported that signals of distress were being fired from the middle part of the Cockle Sands. The lifeboat crew launched *Covent Garden* at 4.10a.m. and found the brigantine *Parthenia*, of Yarmouth, bound from Hartlepool to Lowestoft with coal, under water with her crew of six in the rigging. They were saved by the lifeboat, together with their dog, and brought back to Great Yarmouth. One of the survivors, who was seventy years of age, was severely exhausted and so was taken to the Sailors' Home for treatment.

On four separate occasions in January 1912 *Covent Garden* went out on service. At 7.20a.m. on 11 January rockets were seen in the direction of the Cross Sand lightvessel and, while the crew were being assembled, a message was received by wireless telegraphy that a vessel was ashore on the Sands. After launching, *Covent Garden* was towed to the Sands to find the vessel, the schooner *Falke*, of Bremen, on the Sands with the seas breaking over her. The lifeboat tried to get alongside but the heavy seas prevented her reaching the casualty. She was then taken to windward of the vessel by the tug, where she anchored and veered down. Whilst approaching the vessel, she struck the sands heavily and the lifeboatmen were drenched as seas washed over the boat. However, they succeeded in getting a line on board the casualty and then, by means of the rope, hauled some of the crew through the sea whilst others jumped into the lifeboat. It took an hour and a half to get all of the crew, seven in total, into the lifeboat. The anchor cable had to be cut so the lifeboat could safely clear the wreck, and a tug then towed rescued and rescuers to Caister. Coxswain Haylett stated that it was the most difficult service undertaken by many of the most experienced lifeboatmen.

The third Covent Garden *lifeboat on the beach at Caister with the beachmen who formed the lifeboat crew.*
(William Read, courtesy of David Higgins)

Following this fine rescue, just two days later, on 13 January, *Covent Garden* was again in action. This time she stood by the steamship *Glenside*, of Newcastle. On 18 January, she went to the steamship *Altyre*, of Aberdeen, which was riding with two anchors down but dragging them towards the shore. Tugs were unable to get out of Great Yarmouth harbour due to the severe ESE gale, but at 9a.m. one succeeded in reaching the vessel. The lifeboatmen then assisted to save the vessel and her crew of sixteen and the tug towed her into harbour. Three days later, *Covent Garden* was launched to the steam trawler *Apollo*, of Sandefjord, which was ashore on the Middle Barber Sands during heavy weather. The lifeboatmen boarded the trawler and helped to bring her into Great Yarmouth harbour.

On 28 October 1913 *Covent Garden* worked with the Gorleston No.1 lifeboat *Mark Lane* after signals of distress were seen from the Corton lightvessel. *Mark Lane* was launched at 11.55p.m. and was towed by a tug out to the Sands. As she rounded the Sands, she came across a small boat with five men on board, two of whom came from the steam drifter *Emerald*, of Lowestoft, and three from another vessel which had gone to the steam drifter's assistance. Meanwhile, *Covent Garden* had also launched, reached the steam drifter at the same time as *Mark Lane*, and saved the remainder of the crew, eight in number, while *Mark Lane* stood by. Apparently, *Emerald's* hull had started leaking and although the crew attempted to reach Great Yarmouth, the vessel drifted helplessly northwards. Within a few minutes of the crew being rescued, the drifter sank. After the survivors were landed at Great Yarmouth, the master sent a letter to the RNLI thanking 'the Caister Coxswain and his crew for saving me and seven of my people just in the nick of time, as the vessel was sinking.'

During the First World War many of the rescues performed by the Caister lifeboats were routine, and unusually few were the result of war casualties. The first service undertaken during the War, however, on 9 November 1914, was to the trawler *Muckland,* a vessel being used as an Admiralty minesweeper, which had been stranded on the North Scroby Sands. While the lifeboat assisted, tugs were engaged to tow her off. They failed to get her clear, and so the lifeboat crew boarded her and threw overboard some of her cargo, including ten tons of firebricks. At flood tide three tugs were engaged and again tried to pull her off. This time they succeeded in floating her and at about 8p.m. she was taken, with Caister's coxswain in charge, under her own steam into Yarmouth Roads.

At 8.15p.m. on 5 December 1915, Coxswain Haylett was informed that a vessel was ashore on the Scroby Sands and so he assembled the lifeboat crew and launched *Covent Garden*. Working against the ebb tide made progress impossible, and so the lifeboat was anchored until 2.30a.m. when the tide eased and the lifeboat was able to proceed. Once on the scene, however, the lifeboat could not get near the casualty, the steamship *Inger Johanne*, of Bergen, bound from Newcastle to France. At daybreak, the weather had moderated and the lifeboatmen were able to board the steamer to try to save her. Although tugs arrived later on, it proved impossible to save the vessel as she was full of water. The weather was gradually worsening so the nine crew were taken off and the vessel subsequently became a complete wreck.

During 1917, a number of services were undertaken by *Covent Garden*. The first was somewhat unusual as it was to a submarine that had gone ashore on the Barber Sands on 16 March. The vessel, *F3*, was hard aground, and so *Covent Garden* went alongside to ask if assistance was required. The commander asked the lifeboat to stand by, but by 9p.m. the submarine had floated off the Sands. Coxswain Haylett then guided the submarine into deeper water, where she was anchored while the lifeboat returned to her station.

The final service of 1917 was a particularly long one. *Covent Garden* launched at 9.45p.m. on 26 November after the lifeboat watchman had observed signals of distress burning in the direction of the North Scroby Sands. On reaching the vessel, the 247-ton steamship *Watchland*, of West Hartlepool, on passage with a cargo of coal from Grimsby to Sheerness, *Covent Garden* could not get alongside due to the heavy seas and strong ebb tide, so she stood by. At 2a.m., she was able to reach the casualty and was taken alongside, bumping on the sands in the process. The coxswain and another member of the crew boarded the vessel, and with the lifeboat's help and her own engines she was freed from the sands and taken to Great Yarmouth harbour. The ship was in a bad way, while the heavy weather made this service a particularly difficult one for the lifeboatmen, who were drenched throughout by seas breaking over the boat. The lifeboat was recovered at Caister at 2.30p.m. on 27 November.

The last services performed by the third *Covent Garden* took pace in the early months of 1919. On 9 January she was launched to the steamship *Buffs*, of London, which was aground on the North Barber Sands and stood by until the steamer refloated at about 9p.m. On 19 January, she put out to the steamship *Francisca*, of Hull, aground on the Barber Sands, and found the casualty abandoned. Despite the difficulty of getting alongside in the heavy seas, the lifeboatmen got a rope on board the vessel, and with the help of the tug *Yare*, from Great Yarmouth, towed her off the Sands at about 7.45a.m. The lifeboat then picked up the ship's captain and four crew from a small boat, and both lifeboat and steamer were towed into Yarmouth harbour by the tug.

The final service launch of *Covent Garden* took place on 12 March 1919, when she went to the aid of the 130-ton schooner *Intrepide*, of Gravelines, which had a crew of six on-board. She was launched at 2p.m. and found the vessel an hour later aground on the Middle Scroby Sands in rough seas. Tugs arrived from Gorleston at about 3.30p.m. and assisted in pulling the vessel off the Sands. She was then towed into Great Yarmouth and *Covent Garden* returned to Caister at 6p.m.

In September 1919, an examination of the *Covent Garden's* drop keel by the District Inspector revealed that it was not working properly. The necessary repairs would take some time to complete so another lifeboat, Reserve No.1, was sent to the station, initially as a temporary measure. This lifeboat arrived in November 1919 and in December *Covent Garden* was taken to Chambers boatyard at Lowestoft for a complete overhaul. After a thorough examination of *Covent Garden,* it was found that the necessary repairs would cost between £350 and £450 to complete. The RNLI's Committee of Management therefore decided that, as the boat was twenty years old, a new lifeboat should be sent to the station.

3
Operation of the Station

The successful operation of a lifeboat station is dependent on three requirements: one, provision of a suitable lifeboat; two, the availability of a suitable crew to operate that lifeboat; and three, a place from which the lifeboat can quickly and easily launch. Suitable lifeboats had been provided at Caister since the 1840s, but the other two requirements were less easy to fulfil. This chapter will examine the problems experienced in launching Caister's lifeboats and detail the provision made for the crew in terms of shore facilities.

When the station at Caister was established in the 1840s, a wooden boathouse was constructed in which to keep the lifeboat. The crew's gear was also stored in this house, although at this time the amount of gear was somewhat limited as life-jackets were not in widespread use. By 1867, however, it was not being used and consequently was available for housing the smaller No.2 lifeboat when that arrived. Presumably the larger lifeboat already on station could not fit inside it. Whether the No.2 lifeboat was ever housed in it, however, is somewhat doubtful because, in 1872, a report on the station stated that the house had not been used for some years as sand had gathered in front of it.

It was common at Norfolk and Suffolk lifeboat stations for the lifeboat to be kept in the open on the beach, and at only a few stations were boathouses ever built. As the lifeboats were kept in the open at Caister, a store building was needed in which the crew's gear and life-jackets could be safely kept. A series of these store buildings was built on the beach, the first of which was constructed during the 1870s at a cost of £39 10s 0d. However, within a decade a larger one was needed, and in 1886 a new store was completed by W.J. Walker at a cost of £223 18s and included a waiting room. This store was further altered in 1891 when improvements were made at a cost of £65 15s 9d.

As well as the lifeboat house, the beachmen at many East Anglian coastal towns and villages had look-outs built. These structures were relatively basic and consisted of a simple mast with a crow's nest at the top. Usually, one man would sit in the cabin at the top, reached by a wooden stairway, and keep watch for vessels on the sandbanks and ascertain whether any were in difficulty. The look-out at Caister was approximately 50ft in height, an elevation necessary to see as far as the Haisborough Sands, nine miles off the coast. Having taken over the running of the station in the 1850s, the RNLI was also responsible for maintaining the look-out required by the beachmen who formed the lifeboat crew. The first money spent on the look-out amounted to £3 when it was rebuilt in 1889.

By 1906, the look-out was in a poor condition and so, in January 1907, the Beach Company approached the District Inspector with a view to having a new look-out built. The beachmen considered the look-out as an important part of the station, essential if they were to effectively fulfil their life-saving role. To persuade the Inspector that a new look-out should be built, the beachmen said they would pull down the old look-out, clear the

The watch-house and lofty look-out tower, c.1890, used for keeping watch over the sands. This particular one was struck by lightning in about 1910 and demolished. (John and David Woodhouse, courtesy of David Higgins)

Another view of the watch-house and look-out tower used by the beachmen. (Caister Lifeboat House)

Above: *The beach was constantly under the threat of erosion by the sea so, to ensure the lifeboats could always be launched, they were moved to different sites as the beach shifted. The contrast of this photograph of* James Leath *(to right, foreground) and* Nancy Lucy *(to left, at rear) with the following one clearly demonstrates the ever-changing nature of the sands. The white storeshed stands above the beach, rather than level with it, and the lifeboats have been hauled up the gap away from the shoreline. The boats were also moved depending on the height of the tide. (From an old postcard supplied by David Gooch)* Below: *Looking up the beach towards the lifeboat store with* James Leath *on the left and* Nancy Lucy *on the right, seen during the early 1920s. The lifeboats were dragged across the beach to be launched, but the state of the beach was always somewhat precarious and was liable to be washed away. (From an old postcard supplied by a Shoreline member)*

site and maintain a new one at their own expense. In February 1907 the RNLI's Committee of Management approved the building of a new look-out subject to acceptable estimates being received, but it would seem that the beachmen changed their minds. By June only one estimate had been received, from Beeching of Great Yarmouth for a rather extravagant but very heavy and strong iron look-out that would cost £158. The beachmen then stated that in fact a new look-out was not needed but pointed out that the shed to the north of the lifeboat was in need of repairs and should be rebuilt. The shed was rebuilt on a site to the east of the previous shed at a cost of £30.

The store shed on the beach was built in such an exposed position that it was constantly being undermined by sand, sea and wind. The difficulties of maintaining a building on the beach were compounded by the fact that affordable construction materials at the time were not sufficiently strong to withstand the elements. The store shed therefore quickly deteriorated, even after repairs and maintenance work had been carried out. In September 1909, in an attempt to improve the structure, expanded metal guards were fitted to the windows. However, by October 1911, the store shed was found to be rotten and sand had to be excavated from the building. The situation did not improve and by 1917 was in such a state of disrepair that it collapsed in strong winds. Soldiers and others in the town took some of the timbers for firewood. Unfortunately when it collapsed some children were playing inside, and one of them was killed.

To make night launches easier, a new 1,000-candle power Acetylene Beach Light was supplied in May 1908. The lifeboat was often called out at night and the problems of launching, difficult enough during the day, must have been compounded by the darkness. The *Lowestoft Journal* of 8 September 1908 described the new light as follows: 'The new lamp is provided with a large reflector, and will show a strong light over a wide area. When the lifeboat *Beauchamp* was overturned (see following chapter) the would-be rescuers were severely handicapped owing to the pitch darkness of the night, and it is in order to assist so far as may be possible, rescue work on such occasions, that the new light has been installed.' Six months later, in order to keep the new light well maintained, the Committee of Management appointed someone in the locality to take charge of the beach light and ensure that it worked properly. In November 1909 it was reported that the new light was a great help to the crew during night launches.

Launching the Lifeboat

During the nineteenth century, the era of the pulling and sailing lifeboats, the task of actually launching the lifeboat could take many hours. At Caister, the heavy boat had to be manhandled down the beach and manoeuvred through the often heavy breakers, before getting to sea. The faster a launch could be accomplished the better, but considerable difficulty was often experienced in getting lifeboats afloat. The beach at Caister comprises very soft sand, and on many occasions the erosion or shifting of the sand by the sea made launching difficult. In this section, some of the difficulties experienced at Caister will be described, and the remedies introduced to combat the problems explained.

Beach & Lifeboats. Caister on Sea

The site on the beach at the end of Beach Road where the lifeboats and beachmens' yawls were kept. This photograph shows Nancy Lucy *(left) and the third* Covent Garden *amongst the sand dunes. (From an old postcard supplied by David Gooch)*

The relatively soft sand of the beach could hinder efforts to launch the lifeboat. The sand would often be shifted across the beach to form banks in the area used to launch the lifeboat. Such banks presented the launchers with considerable and often insurmountable obstacles. During the twentieth century, the deterioration of the beach caused great problems. In December 1908, the beach and cliffs were washed away by a gale and the high tide and the beach had to be remade to enable the lifeboat to be launched. In May 1909 the situation had worsened as the foreshore was in such a bad condition. Several hundred tons of sand had to be removed that had built up as a result of groynes erected in 1904 to combat sand erosion. The condition of the beach was so bad that attempts to launch the No.1 lifeboat *Covent Garden* on service, on both 11 April and 28 October 1909, had to be abandoned. In August 1909, the District Inspector reported that it was likely the sand would constantly cause difficulties in launching the lifeboats, and over the next few years a number of solutions was suggested to tackle the problem.

In June 1909, to ease the recovery of the lifeboat, a new capstan was installed for the No.1 lifeboat, supplied and fitted by Beeching at a cost of £15. By July, the new capstan had been satisfactorily installed and sand had been cleared from the gap at a cost of £12. However, no sooner had the sand been removed than it started to accumulate again. The system of periodically clearing away the sand was obviously not satisfactory so in December 1909, at the request of the Local Committee, the RNLI's Engineer and

Architect visited the station, accompanied by the District Inspector, to assess how launching arrangements could be improved. They recommended the construction, at a cost of approximately £750, of an open timber slipway on which the two lifeboats could be both launched and recovered. This slipway would stretch across most of the beach, but roller skids would be needed to cover the final part. Another suggestion, made by the Chief Inspector, was to move the lifeboat to the Parish gap, a passage through the sand-bank from the village to the beach. This would cost very little as the existing store shed and watch room could be moved.

After these proposals had been considered, the general view was that the expense of the Engineer and Architect's proposal made it prohibitive. Therefore, the Local Committee recommended that the existing gap should be widened and dug out. Local labour was employed, at a cost of approximately £100, and the gangway was widened and the sand cliffs trimmed down to provide a good launching gradient. It would seem that these measures improved the situation and lifeboat launching was subsequently carried out more efficiently. The use of skids to smooth the launch over the sand certainly helped, and in 1919 a new turntable was constructed by Parker & Smith. New skids were also supplied, and the total cost of this new equipment was £7 15s. The sea continued to affect the beach, and during December 1926 station personnel were required to implement emergency measures following disastrous beach erosion.

As well as the difficulties that beach erosion caused when launching the lifeboat, another problem occurred when ships wrecked on or near the beach prevented the lifeboat getting to sea. At certain states of wind and tide, these wrecks could present a considerable hazard to the lifeboat as it attempted to get to sea. Their removal was often a matter of importance to the lifeboat crew and also for the safety of the lifeboat. In 1906, the wreck of *Primula*, a brigantine from which the *Nancy Lucy* lifeboat (described below) had saved the crew of eight, was broken up by Trinity House following complaints from the lifeboat crew. Trinity House was also asked to remove the remains of the barque *Anna Precht*, wrecked on 18 September 1906. Although Trinity House was responsible for removing wrecks and ensuring the beach and sea roads were clear, they would often ask the purchasers of a wreck to remove it, as in the case of *Empress of India* in December 1910. Salvagers would buy the remains of a wreck and try to sell those parts of it that remained.

4

The Beauchamp Lifeboat

Although the No.2 station had been established in 1867, the original No.2 lifeboat was still on station in 1891. This lifeboat, named *Godsend*, had been altered and improved in 1875 but by the 1890s was worn out and a new lifeboat was deemed necessary. In June 1891, the RNLI's Committee of Management began the process of ordering a new No.2 lifeboat and, on 15 October, £500 was received from Sir Reginald Proctor Beauchamp towards the cost of the new craft. Built by the Great Yarmouth boatbuilder J.H. Critten, the new boat, at 36ft in length, was larger than her predecessor. Her hull was constructed from American white oak, with copper fastenings, and the gunwale was divided into compartments by three bulkheads. She was fitted with airtight cases fore and aft and had an open well amidships. Plugs were fitted in the bottom of the boat and ballast was provided by allowing water to flow through them into the well until it was level with the water outside.

The new lifeboat was placed on station on 18 January 1892 and just three days later, at a public ceremony held at her new station, was formally named *Beauchamp*. Sir Reginald

With her crew proudly posing in their cork life-jackets, Beauchamp *seen on the beach at Caister. This photograph was probably taken on 21 January 1892, the day of her naming ceremony. Also on board the lifeboat are the donors and various local dignitaries, including the mayor of Great Yarmouth and Sir Edward Birkbeck, the RNLI Chairman. (From an old postcard supplied by a Shoreline member)*

No.2 lifeboat Beauchamp *on the beach. (Caister Lifeboat House)*

Beauchamp, who had given the Institution the money for the new boat in memory of his late father and two brothers, believed that providing a lifeboat for Caister, rather than any other station, was a privilege because 'the men who manned the lifeboat were always spoken of in the highest terms.' After further speeches from RNLI Chairman Sir Edward Birkbeck and the coxswain, James Haylett, a brief service was conducted by the Revd Halward. Lady Violet Beauchamp then formally christened the lifeboat, which was launched with the Mayor, Sir Edward Birkbeck and Sir Reginald Beauchamp on board. Thus, amid much ceremony, *Beauchamp* began her career at Caister.

During her years at the station, *Beauchamp* helped many vessels and performed many rescues, the most noteworthy of which are described in this section. The first service took place on 25 January 1892, after flares on the Barber Sands had been spotted. A yawl was launched and sailed to the sands, but as the seas there were too rough *Beauchamp* put off at 12.40a.m. The lifeboat men found the fishing dandy *Canpida*, of Great Yarmouth, had stranded while returning from the fishing grounds. She was on the Middle Barber Sands, so the lifeboat stood by her throughout the night until she floated off with the rising tide.

On the morning of 31 May 1893, signals were fired from the Wold lightvessel. At 3p.m., *Beauchamp* launched in squally weather accompanied by a heavy sea and was towed by a steam tug to the lightvessel to ascertain where the distressed vessel had been seen. The tug and lifeboat then proceeded to search for the vessel, and came across a Lowestoft fishing vessel which had taken the crew off a barque on the Ower Sand. The lifeboat was

Beauchamp *on the beach with her crew on board wearing their cork life-jackets. The crew, from left to right, are: Coxswain Jimmy Haylett, William Wilson, W. Haylett, George Haylett, H. Knights, B. Kittle, Charlie Snellar, Billy Read, Solly Brown, Joe Julier and Jimmy Haylett Senior; standing in front of the boat is the station's Honorary Secretary Frank Clowes. (RNLI)*

then towed to the Sand and found the barque *Alexandra*, bound for London, laden with timber, about a mile outside the South Leman buoy with some fishermen on board. Having cleared away the fore and main masts, which were hanging by the rigging over the side of the vessel, the hawser was attached to the tug and the barque was got afloat and taken to Yarmouth Roads, with the lifeboat assisting to steer her.

In 1895, *Beauchamp* was altered quite extensively at a cost of £262 14s. Her length was slightly reduced, from 36ft 5in to 36ft 2in, as was her beam, from 10ft 6in to 10ft 5in, while depth amidships was increased to just over 4ft. Overall, she was rather short and shallow, designed specifically for ease of launching from the beach. Two masts, a dipping lug and a standing lug mizzen were supplied, and other alterations included the fitting of four water ballast tanks along the centre line, together with a cable well, deck-relieving valves as well as scuppers; sixteen relieving tubes, with non-return valves, were fitted to free the water from the deck. New air cases were fitted as well as a new iron keel. Various other small fittings were added to bring her up-to-date with the latest advances in lifeboat design. The boat's keel was strengthened and other alterations were made to convert her into what was described as the 'Norfolk and Suffolk improved type.' The alterations were carried out at Beeching's boatyard and, after they had been completed, she successfully underwent a harbour trial at Great Yarmouth on 24 October 1895 in the presence of her coxswain and the RNLI's surveyor, Mr L.G. Evans. Following this, she returned to her station on 4 November 1895.

One of the most difficult rescues performed by *Beauchamp* was carried out in November 1896. On 7 November, the Gorleston lifeboat *Mark Lane* was launched to the 1659-ton full-rigged ship *Soudan* of Liverpool, which was stranded on the outside of the Scroby Sands. By the morning of 8 November, with the weather worsening, *Mark Lane* took off nineteen of the ship's crew but was unable to take off the remaining eight. Fortunately *Beauchamp* had been launched to assist, although in getting to the casualty she had to cross the Barber Sands and shipped some very heavy seas, drenching those on board. The only way to reach the wreck was through half-a-mile of heavy broken water across the Scroby Sands. This was accomplished, although the lifeboatmen lashed themselves into their boat for the dangerous passage. Once *Beauchamp* arrived at the wreck, the Gorleston lifeboat returned to harbour with the rescued men. With the help of a steam tug and through the use of her own sails, *Beauchamp* approached the wreck. She could not get alongside, though, as heavy seas kept knocking her away. Lines were then thrown from the ship, and through using them the lifeboat crew were able to get their boat close enough for the eight survivors to jump onto her amidships. Once they were safely on board, the lifeboat made for harbour and landed the rescued men at Gorleston. Many spectators had turned out to watch as they entered Gorleston harbour. *The Lifeboat* described the scene: 'as the boat made the harbour both piers were thronged with spectators, who cheered lustily.' In recognition of the fine work undertaken by both lifeboats, the RNLI granted £125 to the lifeboat crews and shore helpers.

On 8 November 1899, *Beauchamp* performed another fine service when she was launched to the aid of the Banff lugger *Palestine*. The lugger, while making for Lowestoft from the fish grounds, had got into difficulty in a strong gale and very heavy seas and was stranded on the Cockle Sand. Once afloat, *Beauchamp* proceeded under storm canvas across the Barber Sand. The shipwrecked men had hoisted a small lantern on the mast and this guided the lifeboatmen to them. Once on the scene, the lifeboat was anchored and then veered down towards the vessel to pass a rope to the casualty. However, a wave caught the lifeboat and carried her onto the deck of the wreck, which was sunk on the sand. Although damaged, the lifeboat got clear and the lifeboatmen then succeeded in getting the rope to the men who were clinging to the forepart of the lugger. Using the rope as a guide, the lifeboat was taken close enough for the lifeboatmen to rescue the survivors, all of whom were thoroughly exhausted from their ordeal. Throughout the rescue, mountainous seas continually swept over the lifeboat. Ten minutes after all the crew had been taken off, the lugger entirely disappeared.

Having got all of the lugger's crew on board, the lifeboat anchored until daylight. The steam tug *Gleaner* then towed the lifeboat to Caister where all the survivors were safely landed. It was found that the lifeboat had been seriously damaged by the collision with the lugger and so she was taken to Great Yarmouth for repairs to be carried out. As a result of this service, an extra monetary reward was made to the lifeboat crew by the RNLI's Committee of Management and the following letter was received from those who had been rescued:

Mr James H. Haylett, coxswain of the Life-boat *Beauchamp*,

Dear Sir,– We, the undersigned, being the crew of the Scotch boat *Palestine*, which was wrecked on the Cockle Sand during the night of Tuesday last, gratefully and sincerely tender to you and your brave crew our thanks for the courageous way in which you came to our rescue, and after many dangerous attempts, succeeded eventually in saving one and all of us from a watery grave. We further beg to assure you that we shall remember your heroic services as long as we are spared.
We are gratefully yours, George Mair and William Mair, for ourselves and remainder of crew.

Capsizing of the Beauchamp

The *Beauchamp* lifeboat is best known for her tragic fate. Her capsizing in 1901 with the loss of nine of her crew of twelve is one of the most famous incidents in the history of the Caister lifeboat station. The following is a full description of the events surrounding the capsize, together with details of the findings made at the public enquiry.

Late on the night of 13 November 1901, with the wind blowing a full gale from the north-north-east and the sea very heavy, flares from a vessel on the Barber Sands

The scene on Caister beach on the morning after the capsizing of Beauchamp. *The lifeboat remains overturned in the shallow water, while efforts are made to pull her upright. The nine crew trapped under the boat were all drowned. (From a photograph supplied by Roger Wiltshire)*

The capsized Beauchamp *in the surf. (Caister Lifeboat House)*

This photograph shows the upright Beauchamp *being dragged ashore following the capsize. She missed stays whilst tacking, and on reaching the beach had been hit by a tremendous sea on her starboard quarter. The force of water capsized her, breaking off her masts and trapping the crew beneath the hull. (From a photograph supplied by Roger Wiltshire)*

The scene in Caister Cemetery during the funeral of the lifeboat men killed in the Beauchamp *disaster. (Caister Lifeboat House)*

were seen shortly after 11p.m. and the Cockle Lightship fired the recognised signal of distress to indicate a vessel was aground on the sands. Nothing was unusual about any of these procedures, which had been standard practice for several decades. The lifeboat crew were summoned and the *Beauchamp* was launched from the beach. However, during the initial attempt to launch, the boat was washed off the skids by the heavy seas and was cast ashore. She then had to be hauled up the beach again and made ready for a second attempt to launch.

In the teeth of the gale, with heavy seas running and thick rain, it took almost three hours before the lifeboat was successfully launched off the open beach. After a considerable effort the boat finally got afloat at 2a.m., with the use of the warp and tackle to pull her away from the beach. The sails were set and when the boat was last seen from the shore she appeared to be underway. Most of the launchers then went home to change their wet clothes. Former coxswain, James Haylett, snr, although seventy-eight years old and wet through after assisting with the launch, remained on watch. In the boat were two of his sons, a son-in-law and two grandsons.

Once afloat, the boat proceeded towards the sands in the direction of the distress signals, which were to windward of the lifeboat but as the mizen mast was not yet properly set, the coxswain, Aaron Haylett, tacked just outside the surf. He then attempted to get the boat away from the shore, but, unable to tack properly, was driven towards the beach. The boat was then struck by several heavy seas as she tacked away from the shore. While the coxswain was taking emergency action to avoid the worst of the seas, the boat struck the shore about fifty yards north of the launching place. A high sea caught her on the starboard quarter and she was capsized immediately with the crew

The telegram sent to Sir Reginald Proctor Beauchamp, donor of the Beauchamp, *reporting the capsizing of the boat. (By courtesy of Eastern Counties Newspapers)*

trapped beneath. It was about 3a.m. on 14 November.

About three-quarters of an hour later, cries of help were heard by those manning the look-out further up the beach. One of the launchers, Frederick Henry Haylett, had returned to the lifeboat house after changing his wet clothes and on hearing the cries ran, together with his grandfather James Haylett, downwind to where they coming from – a site north of where they had helped to launch the lifeboat. Here the two men found *Beauchamp* lying upside down, with both masts gone, and waves breaking over her. The lifeboat weighed five tons without gear so turning her the right way up was impossible.

Despite the heavy surf and breaking seas crashing over the boat, and regardless of their own safety in the tremendous seas, James Haylett together with his grandson, Frederick Haylett, waded into the swirling waters. James Haylett managed to help Charles Knights, his son-in-law, ashore after Knights had freed himself from the tangle of tackle. Frederick Haylett then ran into the water and managed to get James Hubbard free. James Haylett went in a second time despite the danger, got hold of his grand-

Postcard depicting the disaster: top, the memorial; middle, Beauchamp *on the beach; bottom, the funeral of the lifeboatmen. (From an old postcard in the author's collection)*

son, Walter Haylett, and helped him onto the beach. Had it not been for the two rescuers, it is almost certain that all of the crew would have perished. Of the thirteen crew who had gone out that night, only three survived the capsize. Eight bodies were dragged from beneath the boat, the last of which was recovered at 11.30a.m., when the boat was righted by a large group of men from the village about eight hours after the capsize. Of the other two men who had perished, the body of only one was found, some days later.

The public funerals of the nine lifeboatmen took place on Sunday 17 November 1901. The Chairman of the RNLI Committee of Management, Sir Edward Birkbeck, and the District Inspector of Lifeboats, Commander Thomas Holmes, RN, were both present to represent the Institution. An enormous crowd had gathered in the village to pay their last respects, and crews from the local lifeboat stations were also present. The lifeboat men who lost their lives were: Aaron Walter Haylett (aged forty-nine), coxswain, and James Henry Haylett jnr (fifty-six), brothers; William F. Brown (forty-nine), assistant coxswain, and Charles John Brown (thirty-one), brothers; William Wilson (fifty-six), John William Smith (forty-three), George King (twenty-two), Charles George (fifty-three), whose body was never found, and Harry Knights (eighteen), for whom this was his first launch on service in the lifeboat. These men left behind six widows, thirty-three dependent children, three other dependent relatives and one partly dependent.

Following the funeral the RNLI Committee of Management, once they learned of the number of bereaved dependents, contributed £2,000 towards the relief fund which had been set up by the Mayor of Great Yarmouth. This fund eventually raised £11,870 which was used to meet the needs of the dependents. The RNLI defrayed the cost of the funerals and compensated the survivors of the disaster.

Response to the disaster

For their courage and determination in helping those who survived the capsize escape from the upturned lifeboat, James Haylett, who stayed on the beach throughout the night, was awarded the Gold Medal by the RNLI, as well as twenty-five guineas, in recognition of 'his great gallantry and of the remarkable endurance he displayed at his advanced age, seventy-eight years, in remaining on the beach for twelve hours, wet through and without food, this being the veteran's crowning act of half a century's life-saving in connection with the Institution's lifeboats.' The Thanks of the Institution inscribed on Vellum was accorded to Frederick Haylett. The valuable contributions of the honorary secretaries of the Great Yarmouth and Caister Branches, Capt. A. F. Clowes and Dr Case, was also recognised by the RNLI's Committee of Management.

One-time assistant coxswain James Haylett, senior, who was involved in the attempts to rescue the trapped crew from Beauchamp. *Despite his age, seventy-eight years, he struggled for over three hours to launch the lifeboat on the fateful night in November 1901 and then remained on the beach while the boat was at sea. He then found the capsized boat and struggled to help the survivors get free. For his efforts, he was awarded the Gold Medal by the RNLI which was presented to him on 6 January 1902 by King Edward VII, Patron of the RNLI, at Sandringham. (From an old postcard supplied by a Shoreline member)*

The large storeshed on the beach used by the crew as a meeting place and gear store. To the right can be seen the capstan used for hauling the lifeboats out of the water. Several storesheds were constructed at this site and this is probably one of the last, dating from the early years of the 20th century. (From an old postcard supplied by David Gooch)

Sequence of postcards depicting the lifeboat memorial erected in 1903 in Caister Cemetery. They show the memorial throughout the last century from the time when no fence was around the site, to a wooden and wire railing, iron railings and finally the railings incorporating the letters 'RNLI'. (From an old postcard supplied by David Gooch)

The memorial to the lifeboatmen lost in the Beauchamp, erected in 1903, stands in Caister cemetery. (Nicholas Leach)

CAISTER LIFE-BOAT

Locally produced postcard depicting The Royal Thames, *showing the scene during the boat's naming ceremony on the right. (From a postcard in the author's collection)*

Shirley Jean Adye *as depicted in one of the various postcards commercially produced in the 1970s. (From a postcard in the author's collection)*

Another view of Shirley Jean Adye *as depicted in a commercial postcard from the 1970s. (From a postcard in the author's collection)*

A postcard depicting the early days of the Caister Volunteer Rescue Service with the newly-arrived Shirley Jean Adye *on her carriage outside the lifeboat house and the volunteer crew ready for service. (From a postcard in the author's collection)*

Recovery of Shirley Jean Adye *on the beach. (From a postcard in the author's collection)*

Lifeboat Day 6 August 1989: Caister VRS supporter, comedian Jim Davidson, is winched out of Shirley Jean Adye *into the RAF's Wessex rescue helicopter. (Paul Russell)*

Jack 'Skipper' Woodhouse on board the hull of
Bernard Matthews *at Goodchild Marine,*
Burgh Castle, during the boat's fitting out on
11 August 1990. (Paul Russell)

Bernard Matthews *under construction at*
Goodchild Marine, Burgh Castle, on
11 August 1990. (Paul Russell)

Bernard Matthews *being fitted out at Goodchild Marine, Burgh Castle, on 30 December 1990. (Paul Russell)*

Shirley Jean Adye *and* Bernard Matthews *on the beach outside the lifeboat house, January 1991. (Paul Russell)*

Shirley Jean Adye *and* Bernard Matthews *on the beach outside the lifeboat house, January 1991. (Paul Russell)*

Bernard Matthews *launching on 28 January 1991 with a film crew on board, as well as the comedian Jim Davidson, for the filming of This Is Your Life, featuring Jack 'Skipper' Woodhouse. (Paul Russell)*

Bernard Matthews launching on 28 January 1991 with a film crew on board, as well as the comedian Jim Davidson, for the filming of This Is Your Life, featuring Jack 'Skipper' Woodhouse. (Paul Russell)

Naming ceremony of Bernard Matthews *on 18 June 1991. (Paul Russell)*

Shirley Jean Adye on her carriage during the naming ceremony of Bernard Matthews *on 18 June 1991. (Paul Russell)*

Bernard Matthews *at sea after her naming ceremony on 18 June 1991. (Paul Russell)*

*Bernard Matthews at sea after her
naming ceremony on 18 June 1991.
(Paul Russell)*

BENNY READ
COXSWAIN
Of The Caister Lifeboat
Tragically Taken
1ST September 1991
Whilst Summoning The Crew
To Launch The Inshore
Lifeboat

HE NEVER TURNED BACK
CALM SEAS FOREVER.

59.3.

*Memorial to Coxswain Benny Read.
(Paul Russell)*

Launch of Bernard Matthews *with the Bishop of Great Yarmouth on board, July 1995. (Nicholas Leach)*

Bernard Matthews *off Caister beach in 1995. (Nicholas Leach)*

Bernard Matthews *leaving Great Yarmouth harbour. (Nicholas Leach)*

Bernard Matthews *heading out to sea from Gorleston. (Nicholas Leach)*

Recovery of Bernard Matthews *on the beach at Caister, being hauled out of the water over skids prior to being pulled onto her carriage using the tractor's winch. (Nicholas Leach)*

Recovery of Bernard Matthews *on the beach at Caister. (Nicholas Leach)*

Recovery of Bernard Matthews *on the beach at Caister. (Nicholas Leach)*

Bernard Matthews *on her carriage outside the lifeboat house on 12 November 1995, prior to launching for the annual Remembrance Service. (David Gooch)*

Trials with a waterproofed Caterpillar type 75C tractor in August 1996. The tractor, weighing 17 tons, is powered by a 300hp engine and is widely used for lifeboat launching by the KNRM, Holland's lifeboat society. (Paul Durrant)

The rebuilt, extended and modernised lifeboat house, standing amongst the windswept sand dunes in March 2001. The large extensions at the rear and to the south provide modern facilities for both lifeboat and crew. (Nicholas Leach)

Four generations of the Haylett family, who were closely connected to nineteenth century lifeboat work at Caister. On the right is old Jimmy Haylett, and next to him is his son Aaron who was lost in the Beauchamp disaster of 1901. On the left is Jimmy's grandson Walter, who survived the Beauchamp disaster, while the child is Walter's son Walter. (John and David Woodhouse, courtesy of David Higgins)

An inquiry into the tragic deaths of the lifeboatmen was held at Great Yarmouth Town Hall on 11 and 12 December 1901, led by Capt. George Richardson, Inspector for the Board of Trade. The RNLI was represented by the Deputy Chief Inspector of Lifeboat, Mr C.F. Cunninghame-Graham, and the Inspector for the Eastern District, Cdr Thomas Holmes, RN. The inquiry team expressed at the outset 'deep sympathy with the relatives of the brave men who met their death in an heroic attempt to render aid to their fellow creatures.' After this, the team examined the background of the station, including how the lifeboat was launched, how the crew were formed, and what kind of lights were used at night when the lifeboatmen were having to work on the beach.

The *Beauchamp* lifeboat itself was also described in some detail, as the inquiry set out to determine whether its design or upkeep was in any way to blame for the tragedy. Built in 1891, she had been used with great success for four years and in 1895 had been altered and improved, as described above. During the inquest, it was suggested that the lifeboatmen had given up attempting to reach the casualty and were returning to the beach having failed to complete their mission. At this suggestion James Haylett is reputed to have said that 'Caister men never turn back', a phrase that has since become extremely famous in lifeboat circles and closely associated with the Caister lifeboat station.

Immediately following its capsizing, the *Beauchamp* lifeboat was taken to Great Yarmouth to be repaired. However, repairs were not implemented and she was never used again in service. In September 1902 she was sold locally but until the 1960s little is known of her. However, in November 1961 it was reported that:

> *The famous old Caister lifeboat* Beauchamp *looks very forlorn, sitting on the waste ground at the back of Gorleston library. The Town Council has contributed to her*

transport to this spot, and now a decision is being awaited as to what shall be done to her. She has been covered with a securely anchored chain mail wire net to protect her from idle damaging hands, and looks rather like a whale accidentally caught in a trawl. Although she is probably not seaworthy, she is evidently watertight for she is half full of water caught in the recent torrents of rain.

After a few months she was destroyed on the authority of the Great Yarmouth Libraries & Museum Committee. Borough Librarian, Mr A. Hedges, reported that he had received three requests for the old boat but he did not consider it was now in a condition for any use to be made of it. A group of Sea Scouts had requested it for training use, a parish council wanted it for incorporation in an adventure playground, and a man from Pakefield had offered to buy it so he could cut it in half and make door porches out of it. 'These people', said Mr Hedges, 'cannot really appreciate how rotten the wood is.' So the lifeboat was broken up and nothing is left of her.

A Permanent Memorial

The first meeting of the organisers of the Appeal, started to help the dependents of the drowned men, was held on 19 November 1901 when local solicitor Harold Chamberlain was elected as secretary. Details of the appeal were announced in the local newspapers, and also in *The Times, Daily Mail* and *Daily Telegraph*. The RNLI made a donation of £2,000 to start a memorial fund, which reached £7,418 within a month. The Appeal fund was closed some months later having raised £11,870, the majority of which was invested and used to provide a weekly pension for the dependents. This fund was exhausted by December 1932, after which the RNLI took over the pension payments for the widows still surviving. The last person to benefit from this pension died in 1986.

In 1902 plans were made to provide a permanent memorial to the nine lifeboatmen. The following year a memorial was erected in the north-west corner of Caister Cemetery, designed and constructed by the London firm of J. Whitehead & Son. Made from Sicilian marble, it was in the form of a broken mast around which the graves of the eight men whose bodies were recovered were placed. The total cost, including erection, was £274 3s 6d and this included £3 13s paid to Great Yarmouth artist Stephen John Batchelor who produced a drawing of *Beauchamp* for the stone-masons to copy. The memorial was formally unveiled on 30 June 1903 by the Mayor of Yarmouth, Col. W. Driver.

A temporary barbed-wire fence, which had cost £2 8s, was placed around the monument initially, but in November 1903 was replaced by new permanent iron railings at a cost of £56. A holly bush was planted at each corner of the surround fence by Isaac Brunning of Great Yarmouth at a cost of £1 2s 6d. In 1928 and again in the 1950s, proposals were made to move the memorial and the bodies from the Cemetery to allow for the widening of Ormesby Road. However, this was opposed strongly by local residents and on both occasions the County Council was not given permission to move the graves. During the Second World War the iron railings were taken down to support the plea made

The fine memorial in Caister cemetery erected after the disaster, surrounded by the graves of the nine lifeboatmen who lost their lives.

A modern postcard depicting the lifeboat memorial erected in 1903. The memorial is still an important part of the village of Caister. (From a postcard in the author's collection)

67

The late Cyril Gadd (centre), one of the station's supporters, presents coxswain Benny Read (left) and Jack 'Skipper' Woodhouse with the 1901 memorial shield after its restoration, July 1991. (Paul Russell)

by Winston Churchill for scrap metal to contribute towards the war effort. New iron railings were erected in 1953 free of charge by Costain Construction, who were building the sea wall in front of the lifeboat house at the time.

More recently, the Memorial has undergone various renovations. In 1988 it was refurbished at a cost of £1,100, financed by the Caister Burial Board. In 1999 funds were made available by the RNLI to have the memorial renewed. As part of the work, some of the stonework was repaired and replaced by Woods of Norwich, the headstones relevelled and the metalwork galvanised by Webbers of Great Yarmouth. The work, completed at a cost of almost £12,000, was funded from money set aside by the RNLI for lifeboat memorials. This impressive memorial can still be seen as a reminder of the bravery of the Caister lifeboatmen who risked and lost their lives to save others.

5
Rescue Work
in the Twentieth Century

Nancy Lucy

Following the *Beauchamp* tragedy in November 1901, the station required a new No.2 lifeboat. The process of selecting a new lifeboat began when lifeboat models were sent to the station in May 1902 for the beachmen to select one they deemed most appropriate for local conditions. Once they had selected a design, an order was placed with the Thames Iron Works, of Blackwall. The new lifeboat was completed in Spring 1903 and on 12 June 1903 towed to her station, by a vessel belonging to Nicholson's Towage Co., with Coxswain John Haylett and five lifeboatmen on board.

In June 1902, the RNLI had received £1,000 from Mr Henry W. Lucy, MP, to pay for the new lifeboat. The MP requested that the new boat for Caister be provided out

Caister Lifeboat, "Nancy Lucy."

Nancy Lucy *on the beach with some of the beachmen who formed the lifeboat crew on board. The group of well-wishers looking on may be representatives of the donor, or dignitaries in attendance for the station's annual Lifeboat Day. (From an old postcard supplied by Ivor Steadman)*

Launch of Nancy Lucy *from the beach at Caister using the haul-off warp. (From an old postcard supplied by a Shoreline member)*

of the money, and be named *Nancy Lucy*. On 23 July 1903, the inauguration ceremony of the new lifeboat was held. The phrase 'Caister men never turn back' had been painted on the stern of the new vessel, and a large crowd gathered for the naming of the *Beauchamp's* successor. Col. Diver, Mayor of Great Yarmouth, opened the proceedings before handing over to Henry Lucy, the boat's donor, who said: 'I can assure you I regard it as a great privilege that I have been permitted to make up for the loss of your old boat by presenting this. My simple duty is to present this lifeboat to the Royal National Lifeboat Institution and I am glad to feel that these brave men will always be at the post ready to answer the signal.' The boat was formally handed over to the Local Committee by Lt C.F. Cunninghame-Graham RN, Deputy Chief Inspector of Lifeboats, and after a short service of dedication was named *Nancy Lucy* by the Countess of Selbourne. A demonstration launch followed and the newly named lifeboat was cheered by the crowds as she entered the water.

The first service of the new No.2 lifeboat took place on 24 October 1903 to the steam drifter *Shamrock*, of Peterhead. The drifter was stranded shortly after 2p.m. on a part of the Sands known as the Patch, just opposite Caister. The Coastguard saw flares being fired, and so *Nancy Lucy* was launched to help. The Caister lifeboatmen reached *Shamrock*, and after standing by for three hours succeeded in getting her afloat. The Great Yarmouth lifeboat *John Burch* was also launched but on reaching the stranded vessel found the Caister boat already there, so returned to station. Seven of the Caister lifeboatmen took the refloated drifter into Great Yarmouth harbour, while the rest took the lifeboat back to station.

A view over the beach showing Nancy Lucy *on the left and* James Leath *to the right, partially covered with a protective tarpaulin. (From an old postcard supplied by Ivor Steadman)*

Perhaps the most famous rescue performed by *Nancy Lucy* took place on 18 September 1906. She was launched to the Russian barque *Anna Precht*, 493 tons, of Mariehamn, which had a crew of twelve and was bound to Great Yarmouth from Borga in Finland with 186 fathoms of deal and board ends, for box and case making. The ship had got into difficulty while making for a safe anchorage. The barque's captain saw the Cockle lightship and was intending to go about when his vessel, caught in the north-east-north gale and flood tide, became unmanageable and was driven onto the Barber Sands. Before a distress flare could be lit, the vessel broke in two and capsized. Three of those on board got into the ship's boat but, as they had no oars, the boat just drifted. The Coastguard at Caister had not seen the barque as the driving rain had reduced visibility and only realised something had happened when they saw a small boat coming to the beach. The boat was flung right up on the beach and the three men thrown out. The Coastguards assisted them and gave them warm drinks, food and a change of clothes.

The Officer at the Coastguard station immediately woke Coxswain John Haylett, who mustered the crew, and *Nancy Lucy* was launched into heavy surf to search for the nine other men from the wreck. They found a piece of wreckage to which the captain and a boy of fifteen were clinging. Some of the lifeboatmen went on to the wreckage, unlashed the lad and fastened a rope to him. He was then hauled through the water onto the lifeboat, after which the captain was assisted on board. The lifeboat continued to search for further pieces of the wreck and soon found another piece of the vessel to which three more men were clinging. They were also saved, while another of the barque's crew was picked up from a third piece of wreckage. The last survivor to be saved by the lifeboat was taken from a small boat which had been launched from a steamer that happened to be in the Roads and was assisting with the search. Most of the survivors were practically unconscious as a result of their ordeal. The lifeboat made for Great Yarmouth, where four of the men who had not recovered were taken to hospital.

Following this rescue, several awards were made to the lifeboatmen by the RNLI. It was recognised that sailing the lifeboat through the wreckage to save the stranded men had been both difficult and dangerous, and the lifeboatmen had displayed great courage. The Silver Medal was awarded to Coxswain Haylett in recognition of 'the excellent seamanship [he] displayed'. Silver Medals were also awarded to Assistant Coxswain John Plummer, Solomon Brown and Walter Haylett, for jumping onto the wreckage to save some of the survivors who were unable to help themselves. This rescue was one of the most outstanding performed in the history of the station.

As well as the endurance necessary for such services as that to *Anna Precht*, the Caister lifeboatmen would often put out to vessels which, as it turned out, did not require their assistance. On 8 August 1909, the steamship *Tarnholm*, of Copenhagen, bound for Dunkirk from Newcastle, stranded on the Barber Sands in moderate weather. The lifeboatmen saw the steamer from the lifeboat shed and so *Nancy Lucy* was launched. She reached the casualty to find twenty on board, including the master, women and five children. It was not necessary to take them off as the vessel was not in any immediate danger, although the master asked the lifeboat to stand by. At about 2a.m. the following morning, the steamship floated off the sands under her own power so the lifeboat returned to station.

On 31 August 1910, the schooner *William and Alice*, of Hull, was stranded on the Cockle Sand whilst bound from her home port to Grays with a cargo of coal. *Nancy Lucy* was launched and, on arriving at the Sands, found the schooner was hard aground. The master declined assistance, but the lifeboat stood by while a tug, which had also come to help, attempted to tow her off. After about two hours the vessel floated clear and the lifeboat returned to her station.

It was more than four years before the services of *Nancy Lucy* were again needed. On 1 October 1914, she was launched to a steamer reported to be on the north part of the Scroby Sands. She soon reached the vessel, which was the steamship *Haller*, of Hull, with a crew of thirteen, bound for London. The assistance of the lifeboatmen was initially declined by the steamer's captain. However, as he was unable to refloat the vessel on his own, he eventually asked the lifeboat and two tugs to assist. A large anchor was laid out by the lifeboat, to which a wire hawser was attached. After four hours using the hawser, the vessel was successfully floated off. The steamer was then escorted into Yarmouth Roads and the lifeboat returned to her station.

During the First World War, the Caister lifeboats performed many rescues. Perhaps the most remarkable was to a steamship in July 1917, a service undertaken with few of the regular crew available and in severe conditions which made launching extremely difficult. The rescue began at 3.45a.m. on Sunday 8 July 1917, when Coxswain James Haylett was informed that a steamer, ashore on the North Scroby Sands, was flashing signals requesting assistance. The No.2 lifeboat *Nancy Lucy* was launched as the No.1 lifeboat, *Covent Garden*, had been temporarily dismantled. Launching was accomplished with great

Nancy Lucy *and the third* Covent Garden *(nearest camera) with the yawl* Eclat *on the beach in about 1910. This photograph shows the similarity of the yawl's hull to that of the Norfolk & Suffolk type lifeboat. (From an old photo supplied by Ivor Steadman)*

difficulty through very heavy seas. The wind was a force seven gale from the east, and the sea was very heavy. All on board the lifeboat were drenched by the time they were afloat.

The casualty, the steamship *City of Oxford*, of Hull, with 130 persons of board loaded with government stores and bound for Sheerness from Hull, was reached at 5.30a.m. The lifeboat was taken alongside and the coxswain was asked by Cdr J. Brown, RNR, in charge of the steamship, to go on board and attempt to get the vessel off the sands using his local knowledge. Whilst the coxswain was aboard the casualty, the lifeboat shipped a very heavy sea and was driven on to the side of the vessel. Considerable damage was sustained, and about 15ft of the port whaling was smashed. The coxswain ordered the lifeboat to be taken into deeper water and anchor while he attempted to help the vessel.

At 7a.m., three tugs from Great Yarmouth arrived to tow the vessel off the Sands. This task was successfully accomplished and the vessel floated at about 9.30a.m. With the coxswain still on board, the vessel, with her crew of 130, was taken into Yarmouth Roads under her own steam. The lifeboat was then taken into harbour and left at Beeching's boat-yard pending survey and instructions from the RNLI about effecting the necessary repairs to the damaged whaling. For this rescue, the Thanks of the Institution inscribed on Vellum was accorded to Coxswain John Haylett in recognition of the fine work that he performed during this service, which had been undertaken with only about half of the regular crew on board. The rest of the crew had been made up from older men and substitutes.

During 1919, *Nancy Lucy* undertook three rescues in the space of little more than a month. At 9.25p.m. on 18 September she was launched to the steamship *Incholm*, of

Leith, which was loaded with 120 tons of salt and bound for Great Yarmouth. The steamship was aground on the Middle Barber Sands, and the lifeboat stood by until she refloated. She then went to two further vessels, both of which were aground but both of which managed to float off without assistance. All three vessels had gone aground as searchlights from the RN fleet moored in Yarmouth Roads had prevented them from distinguishing the usual lights from the town's pier. On 28 November 1919 she stood by the Buckie steam drifter *Emily Reach* (BCK.85), launching at 4p.m. and staying with the vessel overnight until 9a.m. on 29 November. On 30 November *Nancy Lucy* assisted the lighter *Beaujolais*, of Le Havre, which was aground on the North Scroby. Using anchors, the lifeboatmen helped to get the vessel refloated by about 2p.m., and the lifeboat returned to Caister at 6.30p.m.

The last services performed by *Nancy Lucy* took place during 1926. On 9 July she was launched into thick fog to go to the aid of the steam trawler *Vigilant* of Hull, which had gone aground on the Inner Scroby Sand. The trawler's captain engaged the lifeboat to lay out an anchor, and about two hours later two tugs, *Yare* and *George Jewson*, arrived on the scene to assist. With the three vessels helping, and the fog lifting, the trawler was refloated at about 9am. The final service of *Nancy Lucy* took place on 9 August when she was launched, under the command of 2nd Coxswain W. Haylett, to go to the aid of the Lowestoft motor trawler *Qualia*, aground at the northern end of the Scroby Sands. The lifeboat crew found the trawler bumping on the sands in broken surf, so they stood by until she floated off at high tide. The trawler returned to port under her own power while the lifeboat returned to her station. In November 1929 *Nancy Lucy* left Caister having saved a total of 144 lives during more than a quarter of a century at the station. She was sold for £52 10s and was subsequently converted into a houseboat based at Norwich.

Payments, Rules and Regulations

Throughout the nineteenth and early twentieth centuries, the crew of the lifeboat had been drawn almost exclusively from the Caister Beach Company. However, by the late nineteenth century beach companies throughout East Anglia were in decline as opportunities for salvage and inshore fishing declined (described in the section on the work of the beachmen above), and this inevitably had an impact on the lifeboat station. In December 1907, it was reported that changes in the Beach Company during the previous seven years meant that difficulties were being experienced in getting a crew. Many of the men were away fishing in the large trawlers that had come to dominate the fishing industry. The fishermen of the beach company, many of whom had formed the lifeboat crew, had found employment on fishing vessels and could be away from the village for days or weeks at a time. The remedies to this problem included taking men into the crew who were not fishermen and ensuring that payment for launches was consistent. However, payments for launches became a major issue of contention, as discussed below. Paying for the retention of the boat's officers was also essential, and without a reasonable level of pay crewing the lifeboat could become a problem. For example, in 1919, the Honorary Secretary reported that he could not get a bowman because the retaining fees were so low. As a result, the fee for the bowman was raised to £2 per annum and this must have helped alleviate the problem.

Although the crew were volunteers, payments were received from the RNLI for exercises and services. Receiving payments was clearly an incentive for the beachmen to launch the lifeboat as on occasions they would put to sea even when their services were not strictly needed, for example if another lifeboat was better located to reach a casualty. During both the 1890s and 1900s the lifeboat was launched on a number of occasions when, according to the Committee of Management, it should not have been. When this happened, the Committee would withhold payments for the service in question, an action which often resulted in ill feeling between committees, both local and national, and crew. In January 1893, the Committee of Management reprimanded the Coxswain of the No.1 lifeboat for taking her to the Haisborough Sands unnecessarily, passing stations which were nearer to the sands and intended for service on them. As a result the Caister lifeboats were restricted from going to vessels on the Haisborough Sands, a matter which caused much dissatisfaction amongst the beachmen.

In an attempt to clarify the situation, new regulations were introduced in Spring 1901 governing the launching of the lifeboats to the Haisborough Sands in fine weather If Palling and Winteron lifeboats, to the north of Caister and closer to the Sands, were unable to launch, the Caister crew were to be informed. In addition, the Gorleston lifeboat and tug were also to be called out as on occasions getting the Caister boat afloat might prove difficult. When a launch was undertaken in contravention of these regulations, the Committee of Management refused to make any payment. For example, no payment was made for the launch of the No.1 lifeboat for service on 25 June 1901 as, the Committee decided, this lifeboat and the Winterton No.1 lifeboat (whose crew's pay was also stopped) put off in defiance of regulations. The Palling No.2 lifeboat was also launched, although the stranded vessel got off without any assistance.

In 1903, after two years in practice, the Committee of Management reconsidered the regulations and decided to remove the restrictions. The Caister lifeboatmen were free to decide whether to launch in answer to signals from the Wold and Haisborough Lightships in the event of the Palling and Winterton lifeboats being unable to launch. However, launches deemed unnecessary by the Committee continued. In September 1904 and April 1905, payments were stopped following launches in fine weather. In December 1905, the RNLI's Committee of Management approved a new scale of payments for exercising the lifeboat, recommended by the District Inspector, as follows:

No.1 Boat
Crew of twenty men, 4s each (summer), 6s each (winter)
Helpers, lump sum, £3 10s (summer), £5 5s (winter)

No.2 boat
Crew of seventeen men, 4s each (summer), 6s each (winter)
Helpers, lump sum, £2 (summer), £3 (winter)

Considering the relative poverty in which many of the beachmen lived, lifeboat work was clearly an important extra source of income. While exercise launches were held on a regular basis, service launches could not be predicted. This probably explains the men's desire to launch the lifeboat whenever they could, a desire which sometimes brought them into conflict with the Committee of Management. In fact, immediately after the new scale of payments had been introduced for exercises in 1905, the Committee of Management decided, after an enquiry by the District Inspector, to make no payment for the service launch of the No.1 lifeboat on 12 December 1905. Another launch, on 11 April 1907, by the No.1 lifeboat to two smacks on the Haisborough Sands was also deemed unnecessary and so pay to the crew was again stopped. However, £5 was paid to the services of a tug to avoid friction with the owners. On 6 January 1910 the No.1 lifeboat *Covent Garden* launched in fine weather to a vessel seen ashore on the Scroby Sands, but which was not flying any signals for assistance, and so no payment was made for this launch.

Payments for service launches being undertaken to claim extra payments continued to be something of a problem for the RNLI's national Committee of Management. Matters seem to have come to head in 1911. In June, the Committee considered the report of a launch which had taken place in fine weather on 12 May 1911 when several lifeboats, including that at Caister, were launched. Perhaps somewhat surprisingly the Local Committee at Caister recommended that the Caister crew should not be paid for this launch, although the Coxswain stated that the Caister boat had the benefit of both wind and tide, and was therefore the proper boat to launch to the vessel. He also stated that the crew were very dissatisfied with the suggestion of non-payment made by the Local Committee. On this occasion, the Committee of Management judged that the launch was justified and so decided to pay the crew. This decision may have been reached in order to pacify the crew, as the Committe of Management then felt obliged to explain the situation to the Local Committee as follows: 'Although the Committee of Management must maintain the ultimate authority to decide in such cases, they fully appreciated the care and trouble the Local Committee devoted to matters which came under their consideration and in future the would communicate with them when any differences arose.'

Perhaps opposing the Local Committee in this way encouraged the Coxswain and crew to continue to launch unnecessarily. When the No.1 lifeboat was launched to a vessel on the Cockle Sand on 29 August 1911, a launch which the Local Committee considered unnecessary, a dispute began between the Committee members and the crew, led by the coxswain. The decision to launch on this occasion had been made by the coxswain, and while the Local Committee argued no payment should be allowed, the crew felt payment was justified. On 19 September, the crew wrote to the national Committee of Management stating that, until payment had been received for the launch on 29 August, they would not touch the lifeboats. On receipt of this letter the station was temporarily closed and the Local Committee unanimously resolved that the station should not be reopened until the crew had unreservedly withdrawn their letter. The coxswain and crew did not actually go on strike, and in November 1911 withdrew their letter after which the Honorary Secretary authorised the reopening of the station. In this instance the national and local committees stood together, but this incident showed the need for a clear policy on launches to provide a framework within which the lifeboatmen could operate.

Soon after the problems of 1911 had been resolved, new regulations were introduced. Coming into force in January 1912, they governed the launching of lifeboats not just at Caister, Great Yarmouth and Gorleston, but also at Palling, Winterton and Happisburgh to the north of Caister. The rules relating to Caister, Great Yarmouth and Gorleston specified the areas that each station should cover, to try to prevent unnecessary launches. The lifeboats at the stations governed by the rules should not be launched to assist vessels that could be better assisted by a neighbouring station. The Committee of Management explained the reasoning behind the introduction of the rules to govern 'the Launches for Service at the Caister, Yarmouth and Gorleston Stations' as follows:

> *The following rules have been drawn up with a view to preventing the recurrence of unnecessary launches by the Lifeboats of the three Stations concerned. The Committee of Management, while recognizing the zeal and seamanlike spirit of the Beach Companies at the three stations, have felt compelled to take steps to prevent the wasteful expenditure of public funds, caused by unauthorized and unjustifiable launches. In the year 1910 a very large sum was spent in this way, being three times as much as the sum paid for proper and useful services. As the men are well aware, the Committee of Management do not look too critically at duplicate or triplicate launches where the weather is really bad and when there is a heavy sea. But the Local Committees will, with the full support of the Committee of Management, rigidly carry out the Rules, which are issued in the true interests of the men as well as the general interests of the Institution.*

The launch of more than one lifeboat in exceptionally bad weather was clearly acceptable, but the general restrictions placed on the operation of each station were intended to reduce the instances when more than one lifeboat was launched. The limits of operation for Caister's lifeboats were specified as follows:

> North. A line through the Cockle Light Vessel and the North East Cross Sand Buoy.
> South. A line joining the Bell Buoy off the Scroby Elbow and the Middle Cross Sand Buoy.

Previously, lifeboats from Great Yarmouth, Caister and Gorleston had launched to vessels which they had no chance of reaching only so the crew could gain payment. To ensure that the new Rules were heeded, further stipulations were incorporated into them. One stated that if two boats launched because the exact position of a wreck could not be determined due to, for example, fog, any payment would be made to the station in whose area the vessel was found to have stranded. The coxswain was also urged to consult with the station's Honorary Secretary before launching, and to determine more carefully the exact location of the wreck.

No more unnecessary launches were made following the introduction of these rules, although in 1913 the coxswain admitted he mistakenly had the lifeboat launched as a result of confusion regarding the signals from lightvessels in the area. Commenting on the reduction in unnecessary launches in May 1913, the Chief Inspector reported that the regulations had greatly helped 'in checking unnecessary launches and… rendered it much easier to deal with such cases when they arose.' However, the District Inspector noted some problems when he reported to the Committee of Management in February 1914. By this time, the regulations had been in force for two years, but he stated that the allocation of a specific area to a station had not been altogether successful. The rules were therefore modified so that when they were in a better position as a result of the direction of wind and tide, Caister and Gorleston lifeboats should be permitted to go beyond their area, and there was no option but to pay both crews in such instances.

James Leath

With the removal of *Nancy Lucy*, a reserve lifeboat designated Reserve No.1 was placed on station. This lifeboat, built in 1910 by Thames Iron Works for the Pakefield station, was originally named *James Leath*. She was a 42ft Norfolk & Suffolk type boat, pulling twelve oars, and built in 1910 for Pakefield. As she was not a new lifeboat, no naming ceremony was held. Although a sturdy boat of similar design to the craft she had replaced, she weighed almost nine tons, 12cwt heavier than her predecessor, which made launching more difficult. Dragging a nine-ton lifeboat by hand over Caister's beach was a difficult task and attempts to improve launching and ease the boat's passage into the water had to be made, as described in detail above.

The site on the beach where the lifeboats and beachmens' yawls were kept with No.2 lifeboat Nancy Lucy *on the left and No.1 lifeboat* James Leath *on the right. (From an old postcard supplied by a Shoreline member)*

Despite the difficulties of launching *James Leath*, she continued the tradition of life-saving at Caister and undertook a number of successful rescues. Her first service took place on 25 February 1920 when she was launched to the smack *Emblem* of Ramsgate, which was aground on the Scroby Sands. The tug *George Jewson* towed the lifeboat to the casualty, and the lifeboatmen helped to secure tow lines so the tug could pull the smack off the Sands. By 10.30p.m. the smack was afloat and she was taken to Great Yarmouth. The lifeboat returned to Caister at 4.30a.m. on 26 February at the end of a long service.

At about 10.30p.m. on 23 September 1920, the London motor schooner *Admiral Keyes* went aground on the Caister shoal while on passage from Goole to Ramsgate laden with house coal, including a deck cargo. *James Leath* was launched to go to her help. On reaching the schooner, the lifeboatmen boarded her and threw overboard some ten to twelve tons of coal from the deck load. They then assisted with the hand pumps as the vessel had about 4ft of water in her engine room. At about 1a.m. on 24 September, the tug *Yare* left Great Yarmouth to help, but her attempts to get near *Admiral Keyes* failed as there was insufficient water for the tug to operate. As the tide turned, the vessel floated off the sand, and was subsequently towed by the tug into Great Yarmouth harbour where she was beached. Unusually, a salvage claim was made by the lifeboat crew as well as by the crew of the *Yare*. The case was heard by Mr Justice Hill in the Admiralty Division of the court. Hill held that the sum of £250 offered by the owners of the motor schooner, whose cargo was valued at £9,150, was insufficient, and he awarded £200 to the lifeboatmen and a similar amount to the owners and crew of the tug.

At 1.30a.m. on 11 January 1923, the Coastguard reported that signals had been fired from the Cockle Lightship, and so *James Leath* was launched into a moderately rough sea. As the lifeboat was heading for the lightship, she found the schooner *Fred*, of Simrishamn, in a dangerous position with her anchors dragging. The schooner's captain asked for assistance as he was afraid of drifting onto the Scroby Sands. Soon afterwards, the tug *George Jewson* arrived, and towed the schooner to the safety of Yarmouth Roads. The lifeboat escorted both vessels to the Roads, and then returned to station.

The services of *James Leath* were not called upon again for almost three years. She was next launched on 18 November 1925 to the steamship *Flashlight*, of London, which was stranded on the North Barber Sands while bound for London, carrying a cargo of coal from the Tyne. A moderate ESE gale was blowing when the lifeboat launched at 2.45a.m. In fact, the seas were so heavy that they swept over the lifeboat and the lifeboatmen were unable to lay out an anchor from the steamer. So the lifeboat was herself anchored, to windward of the casualty, and dropped down to the steamer on her own anchor cable. The cable was then passed to the steamer, attached to the steamer's winch and using this the casualty hauled herself off the sands. Once afloat, the steamer proceeded to Yarmouth Roads with the lifeboat in tow.

The last service performed by *James Leath* took place on 23 June 1928. She was launched at 1a.m. in a moderate WSW breeze to go to the aid of the schooner *Mary Ann*, of Guernsey. Bound from Blyth to Truro with a cargo of coal, manned by a crew of five, the schooner had stranded on the North Scroby Sands. An ex-coxswain of the Winterton lifeboat had been at sea when he saw signals fired from the Cockle lightvessel, so he made for Caister and upon landing there rang the lifeboat bell to summon the crew. A tug also went to assist, and, with the help of the lifeboat, the schooner refloated later the same day, and was brought into Great Yarmouth harbour.

The three launches described above ended in relatively routine services and were typical of the kind of work undertaken by Caister's lifeboats in the second half of the nineteenth century and the early decades of the twentieth. During this period of approximately seventy years, almost every vessel requiring the assistance of the Caister lifeboats had been stranded on one of the sandbanks off the Norfolk coast. However, by the 1920s, with motor and steam power taking over from sail, the risks to vessels caught in bad weather were reduced and as a result fewer ships stranded on the dangerous sandbanks. The days when Caister's lifeboats were launching several times a year and saving lives and property from schooners, barques and other sailing vessels at the mercy of the elements were coming to a close. Ships powered by engines ran aground less often than their sailing conterparts and those that did could often get off themselves under their own power. Indeed, when the Caister lifeboat launched to assist, she was often towed by the vessel she had just assisted. Therefore, by the end of the 1920s the number of rescues being performed by the Caister lifeboats had dropped significantly.

With the introduction of motor lifeboats at Cromer, Gorleston and Lowestoft in 1923, 1924 and 1921 respectively, stations in between were closed, such as Happisburgh, Palling and Winterton. As early as February 1914 the RNLI's Chief Inspector had raised the question of removing one of the two lifeboat at Caister, but at the time it was thought best to maintain two boats, until at least one of them reached the end of its operational life. By the end of the 1920s, the question of removing one of the lifeboats was again raised and in November 1929 the No.2 lifeboat was withdrawn. In recording the closure of the

Nancy Lucy under a protective tarpaulin on the beach. (From an old postcard supplied by David Gooch)

No.2 station, the March 1930 edition of *The Lifeboat* stated: 'No station has done more magnificent work for the LB Service than Caister. Since the Institution took it over in 1857, its Life-boats have the splendid record of 1709 lives rescued from shipwreck, and the Institution has awarded one Gold Medal and eleven Silver Medals to Caister men.' Although this was the beginning of the era of the powered lifeboat with the RNLI introducing motor lifeboats throughout the nation, it was to be another decade before a motor lifeboat came to Caister.

Charles Burton

With a motor lifeboat newly-installed at nearby Gorleston and the No.2 station closed, after 1929 only one lifeboat was stationed at Caister. At the time of her withdrawal in 1929, *Nancy Lucy* was more than twenty years old, while *James Leath* was reaching the end of her service life and needed replacing. However, the next lifeboat was not newly-built for the station but was almost as old as *Nancy Lucy*. The RNLI had almost stopped building pulling and sailing lifeboats by this time, but had yet to develop a motor lifeboat suitable for beach launching so a motor lifeboat could not be built for Caister. Instead, the second-hand sailing lifeboat, *Charles Burton,* was placed on station. Built at Blackwall in 1904 by the Thames Iron Works, *Charles Burton* was a Liverpool type non-self-righter, similar in some respects to the Watson sailing lifeboat developed in the 1890s and the Norfolk & Suffolk type common throughout East Anglia. She was 38ft in length and had originally been stationed at Grimsby, where she had saved seven lives in twenty-thee years of service.

The first service of *Charles Burton* at Caister took place on 16 August 1930 when she was launched at 6.25a.m. in a moderate WNW breeze to the steam trawler *Jean Dore*, of Boulogne, which was ashore on the Middle Caister Shoal. *Charles Burton* was taken alongside and gradually, with the rising tide and with the lifeboat in attendance, the steam trawler refloated and proceeded south under her own power. She anchored off the entrance to Great Yarmouth harbour, while *Charles Burton* returned to her station.

On 17 June 1931, *Charles Burton* was again in action. She was launched at 4p.m. and stood by the fishing smack *Samaritan*, of Lowestoft, which had stranded on the North Barber Sands, with a crew of three on board. The coxswain had seen the vessel strike the sands as she made her way out of Great Yarmouth harbour. However, when the lifeboat reached the vessel, the Master declined help, but the lifeboat stood by *Samaritan* until she refloated.

The services of *Charles Burton* were not called upon again for almost three years, until 21 May 1934 when she was launched to the cutter yacht *Gariad*, of Cardiff, which was aground and thought to be in difficulty. The lifeboat stood by until the yacht had refloated and continued on her passage. On 7 August the same year she was launched to the Great Yarmouth fishing boat *Handy Billy*, which was in distress about one and a half miles north of the station. The lifeboatmen found the fishing boat about 150 yards off the shore with the seas breaking over her. Her motor had failed and her mast had been carried away. The lifeboat was anchored, veered down towards the casualty and

Charles Burton *launching from the slipway at Grimsby, where she was stationed from 1904 until 1927. She came to Caister in November 1929 and when replaced in 1941 was the last pulling and sailing lifeboat in Norfolk. (From an old photo supplied by Ivor Steadman)*

succeeded in saving her crew of two. She returned to Caister at 9.45a.m. and the fishing boat later drifted ashore.

During the morning of 11 January 1935 the steam trawler *Prosper*, of Ostend, bound for the Orkney fishing grounds, ran aground on the Scroby Sands. The sea was moderate, but later became rough. *Charles Burton* was launched at 7.25a.m. and, although the crew of *Prosper* were in no immediate danger, stood by to refloat her. The Great Yarmouth & Gorleston motor lifeboat *John and Mary Meiklam of Gladswood* was launched, but her help was not required and so she returned to station. At 11.20p.m., with the help of the Caister lifeboat and a tug, the steam trawler was eventually refloated and escorted into Great Yarmouth by both lifeboat and tug. The lifeboat returned to Caister at 6a.m. on 12 January having been out on service for twenty-two hours.

A service performed in closer conjunction with the motor lifeboat from Great Yarmouth & Gorleston took place later in the same year. At 11.15p.m. on 2 October *Charles Burton* was launched into a rough sea, with heavy rain and a gale blowing after flares were seen two miles north of Caister. The lifeboatmen found the motor boat *Beaty*, of Great Yarmouth, which had a broken down engine, in tow of another boat. The lifeboat stood by until another more powerful motor boat arrived to take over the tow, and she then returned to Caister. As she neared her station, a message was signalled from the shore that flares had been seen about a mile to the south east. The lifeboat put about and found that the tow-rope being used to tow the *Beaty* had parted. *Charles Burton*

The lifeboat crew on board Charles Burton *on the beach at Caister, c.1935/36, in the winter with snow on the beach. Standing along the back, left to right, are: 'Clinker' Brown, -?- , -?- , Charlie Hodds, Jimmy Brown, -?-. Standing to the front on the gunwale, left to right, are: 'Bones' Hodds, Virgin Brown, Billy 'Shill' Haylett, John 'Skipper' Woodhouse, coxswain Joe Woodhouse, 'Prince' Green, -?-, Jack Brett Haylett, Paul Barnard and 'Spratt' Haylett. Standing on the beach is 'Funky' Billy Barnard.*

stood by until the motor lifeboat *John and Mary Meiklam of Gladswood*, from Gorleston, arrived on the scene to take over the tow. *Charles Burton* and her crew did not return to station until 5.45a.m.

On 25 April 1936, *Charles Burton* was launched twice to the same vessel, the auxiliary cutter yacht *Mavan*, of Southampton. The first launch took place at 7a.m. after the vessel had been stranded on the west side of the Barber Sands. The lifeboat stood by until the yacht floated off with the flood tide. The yacht then made for Bridlington, while the lifeboat returned to her station. At 11p.m. the lifeboat was launched for a second time that day after the Cockle lightship had fired flares. The lifeboat found the same yacht, *Mavan,* in trouble, this time a mile from the lifeboat station. The yacht's engine had broken down, her sails had blown away, her anchor was dragging and her two crew were exhausted. They were taken on board the lifeboat, some of the lifeboat crew boarded the yacht, and the lifeboat then towed the broken down vessel to Great Yarmouth. The lifeboat returned to her station at 3.20a.m. on 26 April after another long service.

Throughout the Second World War, the Caister lifeboat was called upon to operate under difficult and dangerous conditions. Not only could lighthouses and lightships no longer show their guiding lights, but lights in harbours were also extinguished, and the casualties of war made extra demands on the lifeboat service. The burden on east coast stations in particular was greater than in peacetime: casualties to which the east coast lifeboats launched included aircraft shot down over the sea, as well as ships that had struck mines.

The first service of the war involving the Caister lifeboat took place on 10 December 1939. The Great Yarmouth and motor Gorleston lifeboat, *Louise Stephens*, was launched to the steamer *Willowpool,* which was on fire as a result of enemy action, and picked up thirty-six survivors who had got on board the Newarp lightvessel. She returned to Gorleston with the survivors, and requested that the Caister lifeboat be launched to assist. *Charles Burton* set off from Caister at 1a.m. on 11 December but could not reach Newarp owing to the state of the tide so when the Lowestoft motor lifeboat *Michael Stephens* arrived, *Charles Burton* returned to Caister. Just two days later, on 12 December 1939, *Charles Burton* was again launched, this time to a steamer that had been reported on fire after striking a mine. Although the lifeboat went to her aid, a trawler picked up the five survivors from the casualty and the lifeboat did not find anything, so she returned to station.

At 12.20p.m. on 25 May 1940, a heavy explosion was heard at Caister. The trawler *Charles Boyes*, in Admiralty service, had hit a mine near the North Scroby Buoy, so *Charles Burton* was launched. When the lifeboat arrived on the scene, only wreckage from the trawler could be found, together with two of her crew both of whom were suffering from shock. The lifeboat took them on board and brought them ashore. A doctor was waiting to help them, and they were then taken to Great Yarmouth hospital. The lifeboat arrived back at Caister at 2.10p.m. after what turned out to be her last service at Caister. In 1941 she was replaced by a new motor lifeboat and in February the following year was sold out of service for £100. She subsequently became a fishing boat, but her current whereabouts are unknown.

6
Motor Lifeboats

The first experiments with motor lifeboats took place during the early years of the twentieth century. Some steam driven lifeboats had been built at the end of the nineteenth century, but steam power was poorly suited to lifeboats. The newly-invented internal combustion engine had greater potential and, in 1904, a lifeboat was fitted with an engine for the first time. Although many technical difficulties had to be overcome to successfully operate an engine on board a lifeboat, once these had been solved, lifeboats powered by the internal combustion engine clearly represented the future for the lifeboat service. Initially, lifeboats already in service were converted with the fitting of an engine. In 1908 the first lifeboat to be built with an engine was completed and by 1914 the number of motor lifeboats in service was well into double figures. Further advances in design and development were delayed due to the First World War.

Following the end of the war, the RNLI adopted a policy of modernisation which resulted in many new motor lifeboats being built. Most immediate post-war lifeboats were based on old designs of pulling and sailing lifeboats, and were fitted with a single engine driving a single propeller. As the RNLI gained greater experience in the operation of motor lifeboats, more reliable engines were developed to power larger boats which in turn were able to cover greater areas. In the 1920s, James Barnett, the RNLI's Consulting Naval Engineer, designed a 60ft lifeboat that employed twin engines and twin propellers, eliminating the need for the auxiliary sails that single-engined motor lifeboats carried. Designing and building lifeboats with twin engines was the next major advance in the development of the motor lifeboat.

Fitting engines to the smaller lifeboats that were light enough to be beach-launched initially proved somewhat difficult. Designers feared that the propeller would be damaged during the launch and recovery procedure. However, in 1921, a small 35ft motor self-righting type lifeboat was constructed and sent to Eastbourne where she was launched from a carriage. This lifeboat proved so successful that further 35ft self-righting motor lifeboats were built in 1923 and 1927 for operation at stations where carriage launching was employed. A 35ft 6in motor self-righting lifeboat was subsequently developed, and during the 1930s the 35ft 6in Liverpool class, a non-self-righting design fitted with a single 35bhp engine, was introduced. The last of this single-engined Liverpool class to be built was sent to Caister in 1941.

Jose Neville

Caister was one of only a handful of lifeboat stations to receive a new lifeboat during the Second World War. Lifeboat building had largely ceased as most boatyards were engaged in Admiralty work and RNLI funds were low. When the motor lifeboat *Jose Neville* arrived

A fine view of the station's first motor lifeboat, Jose Neville. *This 35ft 6in Liverpool type was fitted with a single 35hp Weyburn engine which gave her a top speed of 7.34 knots and a radius of action of 50 nautical miles. (By courtesy of the RNLI)*

in May 1941 she was warmly welcomed by all connected with the station. The first motor lifeboat to serve at Caister was far more advanced than any of the pulling and sailing lifeboats operated hitherto. Built at a cost of £4,473 15s 11d, she was provided from a legacy left to the RNLI by Mrs Ellen Neville, of Barnes, Surrey. The new lifeboat was a 35ft 6in Liverpool motor type, powered by a single 35hp Weyburn type AE six-cylinder petrol engine. This gave a maximum speed of just over seven knots at 881rpm, and a cruising speed of seven knots at 800rpm. At full speed, 3.5 gallons per hour were used, against only 3 gallons per hour at cruising speed. Carrying 48 gallons of fuel in total, she had a radius of action of fifty-five nautical miles at her cruising speed.

Not only did the station receive a new motor lifeboat, but a new corrugated asbestos lifeboat house was constructed to house the new boat. This was the first lifeboat house to be built at Caister for more than forty years. The adoption of a carriage launch greatly eased the problems of launching across the beach that had caused so many difficulties hitherto. The new motor tractor also helped by speeding up the launching time, and its use meant fewer shore helpers were required. The first tractor to be sent to the station, which served until May 1944, was T12, a Clayton & Shuttleworth type fitted with a 40hp four-cylinder Dorman petrol engine. In 1944, another Clayton & Shuttleworth type was sent to the station, T16, which in turn was replaced by T48, a Roadless type LA tractor fitted with a Case engine, in 1949. The other RNLI launching tractors to serve the station were T47,

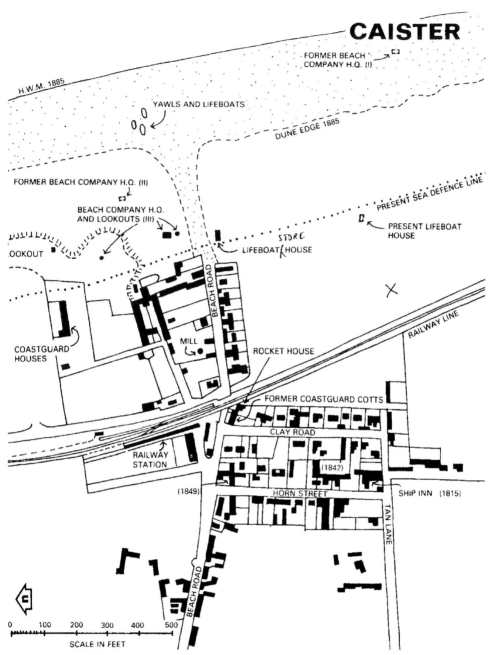

Map of Caister village and beach showing the site on the beach where the lifeboats were kept during the nineteenth century and first part of the twentieth century at the end of Beach Road. The lifeboat house dating from the Second World War was to the south, at the seaward end of Tan Lane. (By courtesy of David Higgins)

The lifeboat house built in 1941 for the station's first motor lifeboat, seen in June 1993 in service with the VRS. (Nicholas Leach)

Launch of Jose Neville *in 1957 using Roadless Case LA launching tractor T48. This vehicle came to Caister in 1949 as a new tractor and was replaced in 1959. (By courtesy of RNLI)*

The Case 1000D launching tractor T72 outside the lifeboat house on a frosty morning probably early in 1964. This 1963-built tractor came to the station as a new vehicle, stayed for two years, and was the last tractor used to launch Jose Neville *from Caister. (RNLI)*

from 1949 to 1959; T47 from 1959 to 1963; T72 from 1963 to 1965; and T76 from 1965 to 1969. Both the new motor lifeboat and the launching tractor improved the station's efficiency of operation considerably. Not only could the boat be launched faster, but she had a greater range than her sailing predecessors and could remain at sea for longer. John Joseph 'Skipper' Woodhouse was appointed as the station's first and, as it turned out, only motor mechanic. As mechanic, 'Skipper' Woodhouse was paid to maintain the lifeboat and ensure it was in perfect working order ready for service.

Jose Neville undertook a number of services throughout her time at Caister. The following descriptions are of the most notable rescues, the first of which she performed in 1943. At 12 noon on 25 June that year, the Coastguard reported that an airman was in the sea 500 yards south-east of Waxham, after an American Flying Fortress aeroplane had crashed. The crew had baled out and all except one had come down on land. As the coxswain and several members of the crew were away, ex-Coxswain Charles Laycock, aged seventy-three, took charge of the lifeboat, which was launched at 12.20p.m. with a scratch crew including three soldiers. A fresh north-westerly wind was blowing with a choppy sea, although the aeroplane had already sunk, the lifeboat crew were able to see it under water so reported its position to a naval rescue launch and then proceeded to pick up floating debris they found. After handing the items over to the police, the lifeboat returned to her station.

The following day *Jose Neville* was again launched to an aircraft, this time a Thunderbolt aeroplane whose pilot had baled out. The lifeboat was launched at 8.45p.m. into a fresh north-easterly wind and found the plane had come down about four miles from the lifeboat station. The airman had been rescued by a small boat which had put out from the shore. At the request of the Winterton Coastguard, *Jose Neville* then went to the aid of another aeroplane, this time a Walrus amphibious type, which had landed in rough seas and been washed ashore. At the second attempt, the lifeboatmen succeeded in firing a line to the plane using the line-throwing gun. The lifeboat was then able to refloat the Walrus and at 10p.m. began to tow her to Great Yarmouth. An hour later a rescue launch arrived and took over the tow. The lifeboat escorted both plane and launch until they were safely in Yarmouth Roads, and then returned to her station.

On 6 January 1944, after the Great Yarmouth Coastguard reported that two barges were aground on Scroby Sands, *Jose Neville* was launched at 1.25p.m. into a fresh westerly wind and a choppy sea to go to their aid. Just over half an hour later, the lifeboat reached the barges, *L.C.M.1144* and *L.C.M.1229*, which were at anchor one mile east of Scroby Elbow. They were lashed together after having been washed off the Sands by the seas. One barge had broken down and had been taken in tow by the other. The lifeboat stood by while they got under way, then escorted them to the roads and returned to her station at 3.30p.m.

At 9.15a.m. on 27 September 1945, a small steamer was reported to be aground on the east side of the Scroby Sands. A moderate west-north-west gale was blowing with a ground swell. The Coastguard kept the coaster under observation and when she was seen to be rolling heavily requested the launch of the lifeboat. *Jose Neville* was launched at 10.35a.m. and found the steamship *Brightside*, of Middlesborough, bound for London. The steamer's crew had thrown some of her cargo overboard and their vessel had refloated on the flood tide just before the lifeboat arrived. At the request of the master, *Jose Neville* piloted the steamer to North Scroby Buoy where she picked up the buoyed channel and continued on her passage south. The lifeboat returned to her station at 1p.m. and was rehoused.

After the war ended in 1945, *Jose Neville* continued to serve the station with distinction. The first rescue she performed in peacetime took place in February 1946. At about 2.45a.m. on 26 February, the Coastguard telephoned to say that the Great Yarmouth & Gorleston lifeboat had just launched to a vessel on the east side of the Scroby Sands, but another vessel was aground on the west side. At 3.20a.m. *Jose Neville* was launched into an east-north-east wind, and soon reached the Great Yarmouth & Gorleston lifeboat which was standing by the tug *Empire Clara*, of Hull. She then went to the east side of the sands, but it was not until 7.15a.m. that the lifeboat found the casualty in a very difficult position, one mile east of Scroby Elbow Buoy. She was the Dutch motor vessel *Caribia*, of Delfzijl, with nine people on board including the skipper's wife and her two babies. Despite bumping heavily on the sands, the lifeboat succeeded in reaching *Caribia* and rescued the skipper's wife, the two children and the crew of five. The skipper declined to leave, so the lifeboat took the rescued people to

Detail from a multi-view postcard of Caister showing Jose Neville *being rehoused in the lifeboat house. (From an old postcard supplied by a Shoreline member and Ivor Steadman)*

Great Yarmouth. She then went back to *Caribia* to find her high and dry, so returned to Caister where she arrived at 11.45a.m. The Great Yarmouth & Gorleston lifeboat went out to *Caribia* the following day to offer further assistance.

At 12.30p.m. on 11 January 1947, a steamer was seen stranded on the Caister Shoal, half a mile from the lifeboat station, so fifteen minutes later *Jose Neville* was launched into a moderate sea, accompanied by foggy weather. The steamer, *Ewell*, of London, bound from Sunderland to London with 2,000 tons of coal, was fast aground on the sandbank. The lifeboat stood by for twelve hours while tugs tried, without success, to refloat her. At 1a.m, on 12 January, the lifeboat returned to her station, but put out again six hours later. Again, however, all efforts to refloat the steamer failed so the lifeboat returned to station in the afternoon. She put out to the steamer for a third time at 10a.m. on 13 January, taking out shipping agents to assess the damage. After examining the steamer, the lifeboat returned to Caister at 4p.m. and at 11.45p.m. that night, the steamer finally refloated.

On 15 June 1948, *Jose Neville* was launched after a series of blasts on a steam whistle had warned the Great Yarmouth Coastguard that a tanker was aground about $3\frac{1}{2}$ miles north by east of Britannia Pier. *Jose Neville* found the motor tanker *Thule*, of London, of 10,500 tons, bound for the Humber with sixty-seven persons on board, stranded about two miles from the station. The tanker's master asked the lifeboat's coxswain to check the charts carried by the tanker. After discovering they were out of date, the lifeboat returned to her station and telephoned for up-to-date versions, which were sent from Lowestoft. The lifeboat took them out to the tanker, stood by her and took soundings. Early in the afternoon the tanker refloated and the lifeboat then returned to her station.

The lifeboat crew on board Jose Neville, *from left to right: Freddie King, Norford Brown, Tom Bullock, David Woodhouse (at front of group), Alfred 'Mabby' Brown, George Codman, and the Reverend John Markham.*

On 8 July 1950, following a routine exercise, *Jose Neville* was on her way back to station when a yacht, *Starshine*, was spotted in difficulties off the north end of Caister Patch. The sea was very choppy, with a moderate southerly breeze blowing, and the yacht's engine had broken down. The sole man on board the yacht asked to be towed to Great Yarmouth, so the lifeboat took the yacht in tow. At 3.20p.m., as the two vessels were progressing, a wireless message was received saying that a canoe had capsized off Britannia pier, so the lifeboat left the yacht and made for the canoeist. However, as he subsequently got to shore safely, the lifeboat returned to the yacht and towed her into harbour. The lifeboat returned to Caister, and the rescued yachtsman made a donation to RNLI funds.

The year 1951 was a particularly busy one for the Caister lifeboat; over the twelve months *Jose Neville* performed six services. The first took place on 17 March when she guided the Glasgow steamship *Southport*, bound for Hull, clear of the Barber Sands on which the steamer had stranded. On 6 May she stood by the motor barge *Glenway*, of Rochester, which was ashore off Newport Hemsby. After towing the yacht *Idler* to Great Yarmouth on 17 June, she performed two services in August, the most notable on 9 August during a publicity trip to the Broads as part of Festival Lifeboat Week. When a message was received that the yacht *Dincyl*, of Lowestoft, was aground on Scroby Elbow, the lifeboat supporters who were on board for the trip had to be quickly landed and the lifeboat put out for the casualty. The yacht had a party of six on board, including three children, and seas were breaking over her. Once on scene, the lifeboat anchored and veered down towards the yacht, enabling a line to be fired to the casualty and a lifeboatman to get on board. After two hours

Jose Neville *on her carriage crossing the beach. (From a postcard supplied by David Gooch)*

Launch of Jose Neville *on a calm day. (From a postcard in the author's collection)*

The annual blessing of the lifeboat on Caister beach, with crew and officials standing in front of Jose Neville *as a crowd of holiday-makers looks on. (RNLI)*

of trying, the yacht eventually refloated and was towed to Great Yarmouth. The final service of the year took place on 28 December when the lifeboat assisted the motor barge *Olive May*, of London, which was dragging its anchor off Caister Point. The lifeboatmen radioed for a tug, and then *Jose Neville* escorted both tug and barge into Great Yarmouth harbour.

The most arduous service of 1952 in which *Jose Neville* was involved took place on 3 December. She went to help the Royal Danish Navy's fast patrol boat *Havoernen*, which ran aground on the Scroby Sand while taking part in exercises with British coastal forces. The Great Yarmouth & Gorleston lifeboat *Louise Stephens* was launched in the morning to go to the patrol boat but could not get close to her as she was high and dry on the sands. At 1.55p.m. *Jose Neville* was launched, reached *Havoernen* at 2.30p.m., took a rope from *Louise Stephens*, and rescued nine of the patrol boat's crew. Four more men were taken off by helicopter. As the weather was so bad, *Jose Neville* could not be rehoused at Caister, so sheltered in Great Yarmouth harbour overnight. The naval authorities subsequently asked if the lifeboat could assist with the salvage of the vessel, so she was launched at 8a.m. on 5 December to pilot the salvage vessel to the sands where *Havoernen* was aground. She helped to connect the tow line between the patrol boat and the salvage vessel, and generally assisted with the salvage operation, transferring various personnel between a Danish tug, the salvage vessel and the grounded patrol boat. *Jose Neville* finally returned to her station at 10.45a.m. on 5 December. Following

Presentation of the Centenary Vellum to the station on 28 July 1957. The two in the foreground are, left, Honorary Secretary M. McAvoy receiving the certificate from, right, Sir Edmund Bacon, Lord Lieutenant of Norfolk. The three crew in the lifeboat, to the right, are, left to right: Jimmy Brown, Jack Plummer and Skipper Woodhouse. Seated, to the right of Edmund Bacon, is RNLI representative Cmdr F. Swann. (By courtesy of the RNLI)

Recovery of Jose Neville *on the beach, in 1957. The wire used to pull the carriage up the beach can be seen to the left. (RNLI)*

this service, the Danish Ministry of Defence presented the Caister lifeboatmen with gifts, and also made a generous donation to the RNLI.

One of the largest vessels assisted by *Jose Neville* was the motor vessel *Maraat*, of Rotterdam, which had gone aground on 8 January 1953 in a calm sea. The lifeboat launched and stood by the vessel until the tide started to rise, and then approached to ask the skipper if help was needed. The lifeboat helped to pull the ship around so she would float more easily on the next tide. However, the lifeboat, having completed this, was unable to continue assisting as she had been damaged by a piece of floating wreckage. Therefore, she returned to Caister, where she arrived at 3.30a.m. the following day. As a harbour tug was not available, Great Yarmouth & Gorleston lifeboat *Louise Stephens* launched the following day and assisted the motor vessel to refloat.

In February 1955, *Jose Neville* assisted a stranded trawler over a number of days during what proved to be a most prolonged service. The episode began on 13 February after the motor trawler *Saint-Pierre-Eglise*, of Boulogne, was reported to have run ashore north of Winterton. *Jose Neville* was launched at 7.15a.m. into a rough sea with a strong north-easterly breeze blowing. The lifeboat found the trawler on Waxham beach but could only get within a quarter of a mile of her because of the sandbanks and heavy seas. However, she stood by while the trawler's crew of 18 were taken ashore by breeches buoy, and then returned to her station at 12 noon. The following day the trawler's agents requested the assistance of the lifeboat in refloating the trawler so *Jose Neville* was launched at 5.30a.m. and helped pass wires from the trawler to a tug. However, the efforts to refloat the stranded vessel failed and the lifeboat returned to her station. The lifeboat launched to the trawler for a third time at 6.45a.m. on 16 February. She laid out an anchor for the trawler and helped pass a tow line to the tug, but efforts again proved to be unsuccessful. When the weather worsened, the trawler heeled over, and as nothing more could be done by the lifeboat, she returned to her station at 3.30p.m.

In 1957, the station celebrated its centenary. A special commemorative ceremony was held on 28 July to mark the occasion. A service, conducted by the Bishop of Norwich, assisted by the Rector of Caister, the Revd J.G. Markham, and the Methodist Minister, the Revd E. Hughes, took place on the beach in front of the lifeboat house. The deputy chairman of the RNLI's Committee of Management, Capt. the Hon. Valentine M. Wyndham-Quin, RN, took the chair, and the Lord Lieutenant of Norfolk, Col. Sir Edward Bacon, Bt, OBE, presented a Centenary Certificate on Vellum to the station on behalf of the RNLI. At the time, the station's lifeboats had been launched on service 745 times.

At 4.10a.m. on 26 January 1958, the Great Yarmouth coastguard informed Coxswain Jack Plummer that the motor vessel *Fosdyke Trader*, of Hull, was aground on Caister shoal, some 400 yards west-north-west of Caister Elbow Buoy. *Jose Neville* was launched at 4.30a.m. into a rough sea with a strong south-south-easterly wind blowing. The lifeboat reached the casualty in fifteen minutes and her master told the coxswain that he had had his engines going full astern for some time but to no avail. At 7a.m. the lifeboat laid out an anchor from the *Fosdyke Trader* and, by heaving on this, the vessel refloated at 9.15a.m. The lifeboat accompanied the vessel towards Yarmouth Roads until her master stated he needed no further help.

Top: Jose Neville *outside the lifeboat house on her carriage, ready for the station's Flag Day in August 1961.* Bottom left: Jose Neville *launching as part of the station's Flag Day in August 1961, watched by a large crowd of holiday-makers and tourists.* Bottom right: Jose Neville *approaching the beach during the station's Flag Day in August 1961. (Photos by Jeff Morris)*

On 13 December 1960, the barge *Will Everard* was sighted aground on the Scroby Sand due east of the lifeboat station. A moderate north-easterly wind was blowing, causing a moderate sea. At 11.10a.m. *Jose Neville* was launched and quickly reached the barge, which had grounded the day before. The motor vessel *Serenity* came up from Great Yarmouth to assist. When *Serenity* arrived the lifeboat took soundings round the barge and, after piloting the motor vessel into position, ran a wire from the barge to the motor vessel. This wire parted, and, just before towing could begin with a second wire, the first wire fouled the *Serenity's* propeller, so the vessel drifted aground. The lifeboat managed to tow *Serenity* to deep water, where she was anchored, then returned to the barge. As the barge was not in any immediate danger, the lifeboat returned to her station after explaining to the barge's skipper that they would answer any distress signals. *Jose Neville* reached her station at 6.15p.m., and three hours later *Will Everard* floated off the sandbank.

During 1963, *Jose Neville* performed a number of useful services, many of a routine nature. On 17 January she helped the Dutch motor vessel *Maria*, which had suffered an engine room fire while in the Yarmouth Roads. On 25 January she launched to the aid of the motor vessel *Crescence*, of Rochester, which was ashore on the beach. The lifeboat stood by while a tug attempted to pull the vessel clear. On 8 April she launched to a trawler reported to be aground on the North Scroby Sands. The lifeboat made for the trawler until a coaster directed her to a rubber float, in broken water, from which was rescued the

Jose Neville *arriving at Great Yarmouth on 8 April 1963 with the crew of eight rescued from the Lowestoft* trawler Kirkley *on board. (RNLI)*

crew of eight of the Lowestoft trawler *Kirkley*. On 22 August, *Jose Neville* stood by the Belgian trawler *Ixous* until she refloated and repaired her steering gear.

The most notable service performed by *Jose Neville* at Caister took place in December 1963. Just after midnight on 13 December, she was launched to the 106-ton trawler *Loch Lorgan,* which had sent out a Mayday signal. The trawler gave her position off the north-west Scroby buoy and requested the assistance of the lifeboat. The wind was from the east-north-east and was gusting to gale force, accompanied by squalls of hail and sleet. The sea was rough with a heavy swell and visibility was poor. The lifeboat, under the command of Coxswain Jack Plummer, reached the casualty at 12.55a.m. and a parachute flare was fired to illuminate the scene. The trawler was seen aground in heavy breaking seas with her bows to the south-west, and rolling with a heavy list to starboard. An approach by the lifeboat on the starboard side, which offered some slight lee from both wind and tide, was impossible due to the extent of the trawler's list. The lifeboat thus had to go alongside the casualty's port side. The coxswain took a calculated risk and ran in, bow first, along the port side. Speed was of the essence if the trawler's crew were to be saved. Coxswain Plummer succeeded in getting the lifeboat alongside the casualty, and bow and stern lines were secured. Seven men were aboard the trawler, and one by one they jumped into the lifeboat.

Throughout this rescue, seas were continually breaking over the lifeboat, which was held alongside the trawler by the coxswain's skilful use of the engines. Once all seven men had been taken off the trawler, the lifeboat cast off the lines. However, as she cleared the trawler, she was caught broadside by wind and tide and was in danger of

The trawler Loch Lorgan *aground at Great Yarmouth on 13 December 1963 after her crew of seven were saved by Caister lifeboat, a service for which Coxswain Plummer was awarded the Bronze Medal. (C.R. Temple, by courtesy of the RNLI)*

Jose Neville *on her carriage on the beach, probably during Lifeboat Day. (From an old postcard supplied by a Shoreline member)*

grounding on the shoal to the north of the wreck. With excellent judgement, Coxswain Plummer put the engines full ahead and turned the lifeboat to seaward of the casualty. Once clear, the lifeboat set a course for Gorleston, where the survivors were safely landed at 2.15a.m. At 5.20a.m. *Jose Neville* put out again after *Loch Lorgan* had grounded on the north beach at Yarmouth. She was broadside on in heavy breaking seas, but with no possibility of reboarding her, the lifeboat returned to station, where she was rehoused at 7.15a.m. For this outstanding service, the Bronze Medal was awarded to Coxswain Plummer. The Thanks inscribed on Vellum was accorded to assistant mechanic F. King, and medal service certificates were awarded to the other six members of the crew, Second Coxswain A. Brown, Acting Bowman R. Read, and crew members D. Woodhouse, G. Codman, J. Brown and H. Pascoe.

The Royal Thames

In the 1950s, a new class of lifeboat was introduced into service with the RNLI. Designed by and named after Richard Oakley, the RNLI's Consulting Naval Architect, this new 37ft design was noteworthy because it employed a system of water ballast transfer which would right the boat in the event of a capsize. The 37ft Oakley marked a major breakthrough because it was the first design of lifeboat that had a high degree of inherent stability, yet

The Royal Thames *enters Great Yarmouth harbour on passage to Caister in February 1964. Note the engine casing does not carry her operational number 37-11, added later in her RNLI career. (Eastern Evening News, courtesy of RNLI)*

The Royal Thames *emerges from the lifeboat house on her carriage to be launched for the station's Flag Day on 3 August 1964. (Jeff Morris)*

would also self-right, a combination that had hitherto eluded lifeboat designers. It represented a significant technological advance, and can thus be regarded as the first of the modern generation of self-righting motor lifeboats.

Because it was designed to serve at stations which practiced carriage launching, such as Caister, the 37ft Oakley had to be fairly light. It weighed only $12\frac{1}{2}$ tons and could therefore be manhandled relatively easily on a beach during the recovery procedure. Although primarily intended for carriage launching, it could also be slipway launched or lie afloat if necessary. The first 37ft Oakley to be completed, named *J.G. Graves of Sheffield*, entered service at Scarborough in 1958. Its success there resulted in further boats of the same design being ordered by the RNLI in the early 1960s, and in 1963 one of these was allocated to Caister.

The 37ft Oakley for Caister, named *The Royal Thames,* was funded from the gifts of Mr G.J.F. Jackson and Miss G. Ellison, together with a legacy bequeathed by the late Mr D.A. Forster, and the RNLI's general funds. She was the eleventh 37ft Oakley to be built, cost £31,749, and arrived at her station in February 1964. The naming ceremony of *The Royal Thames* was held on 14 July 1964, by coincidence also the sixtieth birthday of Coxswain Jack Plummer. Assisted by the Revd J. Jackson, the Revd John Markham, formerly a member of the lifeboat crew, dedicated the lifeboat and Mr G.E. Tubby, chairman of Caister Parish Council, proposed the vote of thanks. At the end of the ceremony, the lifeboat was christened by the Hon. Mrs Valentine Wyndham-Quin. To accommodate the new lifeboat, the 1941 boathouse was altered: the entrance was heightened, the floor of the watch room above was raised and the main doors were enlarged.

Exercise launch of The Royal Thames *using Case launching tractor T72 in April 1964, shortly after the new lifeboat had arrived on station. (By courtesy of the RNLI)*

The Royal Thames, which was the last RNLI lifeboat to serve at Caister, undertook a number of rescues during her time at the station, all of which were essentially of a routine nature. The first two services undertaken by the new lifeboat took place in August 1964. At 2.25p.m. on 16 August, she was launched to go to the aid of a cabin cruiser, reported to be in need of help off Horsey, eight miles north of Caister and the cabin cruiser *Redcap*, a converted ship's lifeboat, was found in a dangerous position off Horsey beach. The cruiser had fouled her propeller and was being driven onto a groyne by the seas. Two lifeboatmen boarded the casualty, attached a tow line, and the lifeboat towed her to Gorleston. At 11.05p.m. on 22 August, *The Royal Thames* was launched to the motor cruiser *Cairnbin* which had broken down with engine failure and was filling with water. On reaching the cruiser, five lifeboatmen boarded her to help control the water. The lifeboat then towed the cruiser to Gorleston and returned to her station at 4.30a.m. on 23 August.

At 7.40p.m. on 12 February 1966, one of the lifeboat shore helpers had heard a distress call from the trawler *Ira*, of Lowestoft, stating that the trawler was aground five miles south-east of Haisbro' lighthouse, and he informed the second coxswain. At 8.08p.m., *The Royal Thames* was launched in a fresh east-north-easterly breeze and rough sea. It was three hours before high water. The lifeboat proceeded to the reported position and found the trawler, over which heavy seas were breaking. The life-saving apparatus team were also in attendance and had passed a line to the trawler. The coxswain fired a parachute flare to illuminate the scene and the trawler's crew of five prepared the breeches buoy. The tug *Workman* then arrived to assist, but attempts to tow *Ira* clear were unsuccessful. As the necessary preparations to take her crew off by breeches buoy were complete, the lifeboat returned to station at 12.30a.m.

On 22 June 1967 *The Royal Thames* worked with the Great Yarmouth and Gorleston lifeboat after an RAF helicopter crashed about half a mile south of the lifeboat station. *The Royal Thames* was launched at 8.05p.m. in a moderate to fresh south westerly breeze and a moderate sea. The coxswain of the Great Yarmouth & Gorleston lifeboat was also informed and the lifeboat *Louise Stephens* was launched at 8.50p.m., and that station's inshore rescue boat (IRB) was also launched to assist. On reaching the area the Caister lifeboat crew were informed that a fishing boat had recovered the body of one of the three men on board the helicopter. The body was transferred to the Caister lifeboat which then continued with the search for the missing men. Various items of equipment were recovered by the Caister lifeboat and Great Yarmouth & Gorleston IRB, but no trace was found of the two missing men. The Caister lifeboat returned to her station at 9.25p.m. The following day, the launching tractor at Caister was used to assist with the recovery of the wreckage. A letter of sympathy was sent from the RNLI to the RAF base at Coltishall and letters of thanks for the services rendered were received by the Institution from RAF Coltishall and HQ, No.18 Group RAF at Pitreavie Castle.

On 22 July 1968 *The Royal Thames* was launched to take an injured seaman from the Fleetwood trawler *Catherine Shawn* which had broken down opposite Caister. The seaman, T. O'Fleaherty, was landed at Gorleston where a Corporation ambulance was waiting to take him to Great Yarmouth General Hospital. The seaman had sceptic burns to his left hand and a temperature caused by the infection getting into his body. When the lifeboat reached the trawler with a doctor, the lifeboatmen found the crew had scrawled the word 'help' in chalk on her side in an attempt to attract attention when their initial efforts to establish radio contact failed. A radio message picked up by coastguards, however, led to the lifeboat launching.

On 2 September 1968 *The Royal Thames* launched on service a few hours after taking part in a mock rescue of the Lifeboat Queen. On the service launch, she went to a yacht in trouble near the Middle Caister Buoy. The plight of the yacht, *Midge*, which was being sailed from Grimsby to Felixstowe, was reported by the survey vessel HMS *Echo*. When the lifeboatmen, under Coxswain Plummer, reached her through a fresh south-westerly wind and rough sea, they found that her inboard engine was broken and a part of it had been lost overboard. *Midge* was towed into Great Yarmouth harbour.

The final services performed by the RNLI lifeboat at Caister were routine ones. On 2 May 1969 the motor fishing vessel *Kaster*, of Lowestoft, went aground in fog near Caister. *The Royal Thames* was launched under the command of second coxswain Alfred Brown to help search for the wreckage together with both Lowestoft and Gorleston lifeboats. The Caister crew found the wreck lying on her side and full of water, with the Gorleston lifeboat also in attendance. One of the bodies of the two crew on board the fishing vessel had been recovered earlier, but nothing was found when the wreckage was searched.

The last service by an RNLI lifeboat serving at Caister: The Royal Thames *enters Great Yarmouth harbour towing the Lowestoft fishing vessel* Winaway *in August 1969. (Eastern Evening News, courtesy of RNLI)*

On 12 July 1969, *The Royal Thames* was launched to go to the aid of the Great Yarmouth speedboat *Miss Britannia*. The speedboat's propeller had been fouled by the ropes of a mooring buoy. The lifeboatmen lifted the buoy's anchor, freed the speedboat, and towed her into Great Yarmouth at the request of the owner, who paid for the cost of the launch of the lifeboat, as it had saved his boat.

On 11 August 1969, the motor fishing vessel *Winaway* was reported firing red flares about a mile south-east of the lifeboat house. *The Royal Thames* was launched under the command of Second Coxswain Alfred Brown into a moderate to fresh south-easterly wind, with a heavy ground swell. *Winaway* was found to be dragging her anchor so the lifeboat took her in tow. The vessel and its crew of four were taken into Great Yarmouth, and the lifeboat returned to her station at about 1.30p.m. This proved to be the last service undertaken by an RNLI lifeboat at Caister. *The Royal Thames* is credited with saving fifteen lives during her five years on station.

Closure of the RNLI station

In 1965 the RNLI set up a working party to consider future operational requirements in the light of changing conditions and the development of new types of lifeboat and other

Last launch of The Royal Thames *at Caister, watched by a crowd of well-wishers and local people. (Eastern Counties Newspapers)*

rescue craft. In 1964, the Institution obtained a 44ft steel lifeboat from the United States Coast Guard which had a speed of approximately fourteen knots, considerably faster than existing types. The new design showed great promise and the RNLI ordered the construction of further boats of this type. As well as this new lifeboat type, small, fast inshore lifeboats were introduced at the same time, and these new craft pointed the way ahead for the RNLI. These small inflatable boats, which required a crew of only two, had been introduced in response to the increasing number of inshore incidents in relatively calm weather to which lifeboats were being called. Their speed made them the ideal craft to assist the increasing number of people who were using the sea for leisure. They could be launched quickly, and at sea could reach a speed of twenty knots.

As a result of the changes in casualty patterns and the new rescue craft available for service, the RNLI's working party recommended a number of changes to the operational deployment of lifeboats. These involved the introduction of inshore lifeboats in place of offshore craft at various stations, such as Minehead and Weston-super-Mare. Several fast 44ft steel lifeboats, which became known as the 'Waveney' class, were built during the late 1960s and soon entered service. In 1967, the second of the class, *Khami*, was placed on station at Great Yarmouth & Gorleston. Its greater speed meant coverage of the area by the Gorleston lifeboat was improved. This area included the seas around Caister, to the north of Great Yarmouth, which could be covered more quickly and effectively than by the previous lifeboat. The Institution therefore decided that a lifeboat at Caister was no longer needed and in October 1969 the RNLI lifeboat was withdrawn and the station closed. During the RNLI's involvement with the station, between 1857 and 1969, the Caister lifeboats saved 1,814 lives.

The final launch of an RNLI lifeboat from the beach at Caister took place on Friday 24 October 1969. In bright autumn sunshine, watched by people from the village and about 150 local children, *The Royal Thames* was taken out of the lifeboat house for the last time. She was manned by the same crew that brought her from Cowes five years previously: Coxswain Plummer, who had been awarded the British Empire Medal in the Queens Birthday Honours in June, former Coxswain J. Brown, mechanic 'Skipper' Woodhouse, and the honorary secretary Mr M. McAvoy. Before the launch, Coxswain Plummer took down the plaques from above the boathouse doors. The boat was pushed across the beach by the tractor for the last time, with children from Caister Junior School cheering as she went. After a routine launch, the lifeboat turned south on her final journey as Caister Lifeboat. She was taken to Fletcher's boatyard at Oulton Broad, Lowestoft, where she was overhauled prior to being reallocated to the Runswick station in Yorkshire. She served at Runswick until 1978, and was then stationed at Pwllheli from 1979 to 1991.

The last launch was supervised by the RNLI's District Inspector, Cdr D. Wilford, and Mr C. Wilkinson from the RNLI's Depot at Boreham Wood. After the boat had gone, they began the task of clearing out the lifeboat house. The now redundant lifejackets were bundled into a large box and taken away, together with ropes and other equipment that was not required. The boathouse doors were then closed on more than a century of life-saving from Caister beach. At the time of the final launch, a certain degree of inevitability about the event was felt amongst the local people. Coxswain Plummer summed up local feelings when he said 'I am sorry, but you have got to move with the times. I am disappointed but one has to take a realistic view of these things.' However, despite this realistic outlook and the considerable sadness that accompanied the RNLI's withdrawal, a new chapter in the history of life-saving at Caister was about to be opened and a new, unique organisation established.

7
The Volunteer Rescue Service

The RNLI decision to withdraw the Caister lifeboat, announced several months prior to the boat's actual departure in October 1969, stunned many people in the village. Chairman of the Caister Parish Council, Mr Chase, summed up local feelings when he said: 'It's worse than London losing Trafalgar Square. We are all very sad.' Coxswain Plummer was shocked by the suddenness of the decision. 'Skipper' Woodhouse, station mechanic since 1941, was dismayed by the news: 'I can't believe it's happening. There will be people drown if we don't have a boat at Caister.' Local feeling was clearly running high. Nobody in the village believed that the station should have been closed, so moves were made to continue a lifeboat service of some kind. Local resources were used and the necessary finance was raised through local initiatives. A public meeting was called in the village and a committee of ten appointed to examine the possibility of running an independently-operated volunteer lifeboat. With relatively modest aims initially, the Caister Volunteer Rescue Service (CVRS) was established as a group of determined local people set about maintaining the tradition of life-saving at Caister.

The new committee immediately began raising funds so that an offshore lifeboat could be provided. The lifeboat house, which belonged to the County Borough of Great Yarmouth following the RNLI's withdrawal, was rented to the CVRS at a peppercorn rent. The RNLI left the caterpillar-tracked launching carriage, a set of oilskins and several other pieces of equipment, which the new organisation soon put to use. Former mechanic 'Skipper' Woodhouse provided his 16ft fibreglass dinghy, equipped with an outboard engine, so that a rescue service, albeit of a rather limited nature, was maintained. An inflatable inshore rescue boat was soon provided, funded by Caister school children, who undertook a charity walk to raise the necessary money. During the mid-1970s, an organisation known as the Friends of Caister Lifeboat was formed, and its members have since provided much finance to ensure the station remains fully operational.

The two boats operated at Caister during the first years of the CVRS performed a number of rescues in the early 1970s, albeit in moderate sea conditions. The first time they were called upon was the morning of 15 March 1970. Lloyd's agents requested that the rescue boat take the Master and Mate of the Dutch motor vessel *Interwave*, of Groningen, back to their ship, which was aground on the Scroby Sands. They had been lifted off two days before by helicopter while the rest of the crew had been taken off by lifeboats from Gorleston and Lowestoft. The rescue boat was manned on this occasion by a crew of three, and the salvage money of just over £50 went straight to CVRS funds.

The bottle breaks over the bow of Shirley Jean Adye *to formally christen the new lifeboat on 5 August 1973. (Caister Lifeboat House)*

Shirley Jean Adye

The CVRS gradually raised sufficient funds to purchase a lifeboat. Although the Service originally intended to have a boat built and designed specifically for the station, in the end this proved unrealistic and so an ex-RNLI lifeboat was purchased in 1973 at a cost of £4,500. The boat, a twin-engined 35ft 6in Liverpool type, similar in design to the station's lifeboat of 1940, *Jose Neville*, had been built in 1953 and was named *W. Ross MacArthur of Glasgow* when in service with the RNLI. After serving at the St Abbs station in the Scottish Borders for eleven years, she was sold out of RNLI service in 1968 to David Case, of Fakenham, who used her as a fishing vessel operating out of Wells-next-the-Sea where Case was the honorary secretary of the local RNLI lifeboat station. The CVRS bought her from him during 1973 and in July that year the International D8 launching tractor arrived, bought at a further cost of £3,850.

On 5 August 1973, the newly-acquired lifeboat was formally renamed *Shirley Jean Adye* at a ceremony held outside the lifeboat house at Caister. In spite of the rain, hundreds of people were present for the occasion to support the CVRS. The funding for the boat

Shirley Jean Adye is launched at the end of her naming ceremony watched by a large crowd of well-wishers. (Caister Lifeboat House)

had come entirely from local donations and the efforts of the people in the village. The largest donation, amounting to £1,000, had been received from British Petroleum. The CVRS showed its appreciation by inviting the BP manager for the Great Yarmouth area, Mr A.M. Adye, to suggest a name for the new boat – he chose his wife's. When Mrs Adye arrived at Caister on 5 August to name the new boat, she was unaware after whom it was to be named and was therefore surprised when the name was revealed.

CVRS Chairman, Mr D. Shaw, oversaw the proceedings, and after welcoming Mrs Adye and the other guests, who included representatives from Sheringham, Cromer and Wells lifeboat stations, he spoke of the need to carry on the tradition of life-saving after the departure of the RNLI in 1969. Between then and the ceremony, he said that the station's temporary rescue boats had saved twelve lives, and that the station wanted to work alongside RNLI lifeboats. As if to emphasise this desire, the Gorleston lifeboat *Khami* was at anchor just off the beach having been invited to attend the ceremony. A service of dedication was then held, conducted by the Revd J.R. Lusty, minister of Caister Beach Road Methodist Church, assisted by the Rector of Caister, the Revd R.R. Dommitt. After the dedication, Coxswain Alfred 'Mabby' Brown and his crew, together with various CVRS officials, took *Shirley Jean Adye* to sea for a demonstration run and an exercise with the SAR helicopter, which arrived at the end of the ceremony.

At the time of the naming of the 'new' lifeboat, the CVRS still owed a considerable amount of money. However, by the mid-1970s all outstanding monies owing on the lifeboat, as well as on the launching tractor and the other items of equipment needed to get the station operational, had been paid off. The financial success of the CVRS was the

Launch of Shirley Jean Adye *during the 1970s. (From a postcard in the author's collection)*

result of considerable fund-raising efforts made since 1969. Although money for the lifeboat had been raised locally, donations had been received from all over the country, and the organisation enjoyed publicity on a national level.

The newly-operational Caister lifeboat was soon in action; the first service performed by *Shirley Jean Adye* took place on 17 August 1973. She was launched at 4.45p.m. to go to the aid of the passenger boat *John and Doris*, which was aground on the Scroby Sand with a number of passengers on board. The Great Yarmouth & Gorleston lifeboat *Khami* had taken off the passengers, sixteen in total, leaving the owner on board. With the assistance of *Shirley Jean Adye*, the vessel was refloated by 7p.m. and escorted to Great Yarmouth. *Shirley Jean Adye* then returned to her station and was recovered at 8.30p.m.

Several more services were undertaken in 1973. On 25 October, *Shirley Jean Adye* was launched at 2.30a.m. with Second Coxswain David Woodhouse in command after red flares had been sighted off Caister. The lifeboatmen found the motor yacht *White Heather*, with three on board, aground on Caister Shoal, west-south-west of the Mid Caister Buoy. A tow line was attached to the casualty, but after about fifteen minutes of towing without result, the lifeboat went alongside to change the tow position. After a further three-quarters of an hour, the lifeboat succeeded in towing the vessel clear. The casualty's engines had been stopped while she was grounded as she was leaking, and so the lifeboat towed her into Great Yarmouth harbour, then returned to station at 7a.m.

During the early years of its operation, the service had to become recognised as a rescue unit by the Coastguards. Once this had been achieved, and with an offshore lifeboat in place, Great Yarmouth Coastguard soon began calling on the Caister volunteers regularly. Not only were they working well with the Coastguard, but the crew also organised exercises with the RNLI lifeboat at Gorleston. By 1975, when some Caister crew members went out on exercise with the Great Yarmouth & Gorleston lifeboat *Khami*, and the Gorleston crew were invited out for an exercise with the Caister lifeboat, the lifeboat at Caister had become recognised as one of the rescue units on the East Anglian coast.

On 28 December 1978 the difficulties and dangers of launching a lifeboat from a carriage off the open beach at Caister were starkly demonstrated. *Shirley Jean Adye* was being launched during the evening to investigate the sighting of red flares when she was hit by a heavy sea that pulled her off the launching carriage. She was hurled broadside onto the beach, the sea broke completely over her, and the crew found themselves up to their chests in icy water. The heavy sea, which broke the fore-ropes securing the lifeboat to the carriage, came amidships and the boat was immediately filled with water. Conditions, as the lifeboat was prepared for launching, were later described as terrible by Coxswain Alfred Brown. He explained: 'We had the boat in the sea and don't exactly know what happened then. A huge sea broke over us and threw us back on the beach and we lost the carriage.'

The lifeboat remained undamaged despite the power of the sea, but the launching carriage was swept away. The carriage, an expensive and essential piece of equipment, was lost and meant the lifeboat was out of action, albeit temporarily. An extensive search for the carriage was mounted. However, it was not until 7 January 1979 that it was found, half-buried beneath the sand approximately fifteen yards from the water's edge, by a team from Decca Survey using the charter boat *York Enterprise*. Although its location was known, the problem of recovering the carriage, in what was a costly operation, had to be overcome and several months passed before the Dutch salvage company Smit-Tak was asked to help. Using their ship *Dolfun*, the Dutch salvage crew succeeded in lifting the sunken carriage which, although having been submerged in the sand and sea for six months, was not damaged. The salvage crew generously decided not to charge for the operation, reported to have cost around £20,000. This decision was explained by salvage officer Pieter Pardoen: 'We agreed to do the job when we were first approached. But then we thought that maybe one day we would need the lifeboat ourselves and we decided to do it for free.' After the tricky salvage operation had been completed, the lifeboat resumed service following her enforced and unfortunate period of inaction.

The only service undertaken during 1979, and the first for almost a year, was a long one for the Caister lifeboatmen. On 4 December *Shirley Jean Adye* was launched to the 255-ton Lowestoft trawler *Suffolk Chieftain* which had run aground on the Scroby Sands. The lifeboat succeeded in taking off the trawler's crew of eleven and landed them at Great Yarmouth. The vessel was returning from a fishing trip when she grounded, and, despite efforts to free her, she remained fast. The following day, *Shirley Jean Adye* was again launched and this time took the trawler's skipper and engineer back to the vessel, and assisted in refloating her. The trawler's engines were started and she was freed without difficulty. The lifeboat then escorted her back to Lowestoft before returning to station.

One of the most notable services performed by the Caister lifeboat in the era of the Volunteer Rescue Service took place on 18 November 1986. At about 11.15p.m. that day, crew member Paul Durrant picked up a radio message from the supply vessel *Seaforth Conqueror* which she was aground on the North Scroby Sand, east of Caister Buoy, and in difficulty. Within minutes, the maroons were fired and *Shirley Jean Adye* was launched into what Coxswain Benny Read described as the worst conditions he had known for more

Shirley Jean Adye on the beach outside the lifeboat house, with the first CVRS tractor, on the annual Raft Race day, 26 August 1984. (David Higgins)

than thirty years. Just after midnight, the supply vessel's crew decided to abandon ship. The Great Yarmouth & Gorleston lifeboat *Barham* arrived on the scene at about 12.05a.m. and stood by illuminating the scene by searchlight and parachute flares. Caister lifeboat was then taken alongside and managed to get eight members of the supply vessel's crew off, getting clear of the casualty by 1.30a.m. According to Coxswain Read, 'As she went up [on the crest of a wave] we pulled one of the crew on to the lifeboat before she dropped 10 or 15 feet into the next trough.' It was the worst seas experienced by Read, who felt the lifeboat's crew were lucky not to have suffered serious injuries.

Once the Caister lifeboat had taken off eight of the crew, the Gorleston lifeboat took off the Master and Engineer. During the approach, *Barham* hit the bottom twice and had to withdraw before another more successful approach was made. The two lifeboats then made for Gorleston harbour to land the survivors, arriving at 3a.m. At 6a.m. *Shirley Jean Adye* left Gorleston with the supply vessel's Master and five of the crew. After the rescue, it was presumed that the casualty would break its plates on the bottom and sink. However, the vessel survived and so the Caister lifeboat took the crew back to the ship, which was riding at anchor. After taking depth soundings the crew restarted the engines, and, with two Caister lifeboatmen on board, slipped the anchor. The vessel pulled away from the sands and was anchored in the Roads. The two members of the lifeboat crew were subsequently lifted off the ship by an RAF helicopter and returned to Caister beach. Following

Shirley Jean Adye *on the beach with the inshore lifeboat, August 1986. (Paul Russell)*

this outstanding service, the Thanks Inscribed on Vellum was accorded to Coxswain Benny Read by the RNLI, and Vellum Service Certificates were presented to the lifeboat crew, which consisted of James Weddall, Malcolm Dyble, Colin Richmond, Donald Griffin and Michael Nutt. The Thanks on Vellum was also accorded to the Gorleston Coxswain/Mechanic Richard Hawkins, and Vellum service certificates were presented to the Gorleston lifeboatmen by the RNLI District Inspector, Tom Nutman.

The service to *Seaforth Conqueror* showed the continuing necessity of the Caister lifeboat, although by the late 1980s Shirley *Jean Adye* was beginning to show her age. Despite an extensive refit at Great Yarmouth, during which new engines were fitted and the boat was completely overhauled at a cost of approximately £20,000, a new and modern lifeboat was needed for the station. The CVRS therefore formed an Appeal Committee whose sole aim was to raise funds for a new lifeboat. On 23 April 1987 the Appeal was formally launched by the Mayor of Great Yarmouth and Michelle Newman, BBC Look East presenter, with an ambitious target of £400,000 to provide a more modern and faster lifeboat for the station. The support and publicity for the Appeal was considerable. During the next four years, Skipper Jack Woodhouse appeared twice on the Wogan television chat show, while entertainers Russ Abbott and Bobby Davro took part in a life-saving display and supported a charity event during the 1987 summer season. One of the highpoints of the appeal came in 1988 when HRH Prince Charles visited the station and was taken out for a trip on board *Shirley Jean Adye* with Coxswain Benny Read and his crew.

Launch of Shirley Jean Adye *on exercise in August 1985. (Jeff Morris)*

Shirley Jean Adye *off Caister beach in August 1985. (Jeff Morris)*

HRH Prince Charles at Caister in 1988 with Coxswain Benny Read and his crew. (Caister Lifeboat House)

Meanwhile, life-saving from Caister continued. On 2 April 1987, *Shirley Jean Adye* was launched at 12.30a.m. to the 52ft motor vessel *Akelda*, of Guernsey, which had gone aground off Horsey beach in moderate seas, while on passage from Poole to Grimsby. The lifeboat stood by throughout the night, and at daybreak managed to get a line aboard the casualty. The first line broke, but a second was connected and, although it pulled a bollard off the motor vessel's deck, it held fast to the anchor chain and the vessel was refloated with the assistance of the Lowestoft-based tug *Anglian* after being aground for eleven hours. Commenting on the service, Coxswain Benny Read said: 'We couldn't do much all night because it was low water and she was high and dry. It was a cold and horrible night, raining and blowing.'

The final services undertaken by *Shirley Jean Adye* took place in 1990. On 3 May, she towed the motor fishing vessel *Beryl Ann*, of Lowestoft, back to her home port after the vessel had broken down north of Mundesley. On 25 May, she went to another fishing vessel, the ex-lifeboat *Ann Isabella*, which was towed into Lowestoft. *Shirley Jean Adye's* 88th and final service launch as Caister lifeboat came on 9 September 1990. She was launched at 8.35p.m. to the yacht *Contessa* which had engine trouble off Winterton. The yacht was taking in a small amount of water and the engine would not start, so the lifeboat towed the yacht into Great Yarmouth. The two vessels entered the harbour at about 10.15p.m. and the lifeboat returned to her station shortly after midnight.

The Avon single-engined inshore lifeboat used by the CVRS during the 1980s. (Paul Russell)

Shirley Jean Adye *approaching the beach on 2 August 1987 to be recovered. (Paul Russell)*

Bernard Matthews *being fitted out at Goodchild Marine, Burgh Castle, on 30 December 1990. (Paul Russell)*

Bernard Matthews

As a result of the tremendous fund-raising activities in and around Caister during the late 1980s, the CVRS Appeal Committee was in a strong financial position. The members of the committee were therefore able to take the first steps in obtaining a new lifeboat and purchased the hull of a 38ft Lochin type vessel from Lochin Marine, a small boatbuilder based at Rye in Sussex. The yard had already designed and built a 33ft lifeboat for the RNLI, known as the Brede class, and the hull of the new lifeboat was an extended version of the Brede. Once the hull had been obtained, it needed to be fitted out and equipped as a lifeboat. The contract to fit out the hull as a lifeboat was awarded to a local yard, Goodchild Marine, based at Burgh Castle, while another local firm, LEC Marine, agreed to carry out the electrical contract free of labour charges. Work on fitting out began on 26 September 1989.

After the new lifeboat had been completed at Goodchild's yard, she underwent a series of trials which she passed with flying colours, and was then ready to go on station. She arrived at Caister at 3p.m. on 15 May 1991, exactly fifty years after the first motor lifeboat was placed on station. The new lifeboat, based on the Lochin Marine design, was 38ft 6in in length and 13ft in breadth. Weighing twelve tons, she was powered by twin 280hp Ford Sabre diesel engines which give her a speed of eighteen knots and a range of 220 nautical miles. Her equipment included twin echo sounders, a survivors cabin for eight people, VHF direction finder, Decca navigator, fire-fighting equipment and the controls were duplicated on the bridge.

By the time the lifeboat had been ordered, the Appeal had gained a high public profile. Norfolk turkey farmer Bernard Matthews pledged his support and the Anglia TV documentary 'Keep the boat afloat' further raised public awareness. During 1990 fund-raising activities continued, and in the summer comedian Jim Davidson became involved in the Appeal. He organised end-of-the-pier shows at Great Yarmouth and bought a new inshore lifeboat for the station as a result. However there were some surprises still to come. On 28 January 1991 Michael Aspel stowed away on the new lifeboat during its trials to spring a 'This Is Your Life' surprise on Skipper Woodhouse. The show was held at the Marina, Great Yarmouth, before an audience of specially invited guests, and the new boat was shown on stage as part of the backdrop. Another appearance on national TV by Skipper further raised public awareness of the independent lifeboat station and helped to boost the Appeal.

The culmination of the Appeal Committee's hard work and planning was the formal naming ceremony and dedication of the new boat which took place on 18 June 1991. Harry Barker, chairman of the Appeal, opened the proceedings and presented the keys of the new lifeboat to Colin Goodley, chairman of the CVRS. The Revd John Markham, a former member of the lifeboat crew, then dedicated the lifeboat, assisted by the Revd Richard Dommett, a former chairman, the Revd Edwin Sutton and Capt. Kenneth Hawkins. Following the formal ceremony, the new lifeboat was christened *Bernard Matthews* by HRH Princess Alexandra, in recognition of the generous support given by Bernard Matthews. At the end of the ceremony the new lifeboat was launched to demon-strate to the assembled crowd her capabilities at sea.

The first rescue performed by the new lifeboat took place on 18 July 1991. She was launched to escort the broken down fishing vessel *David John*, which was being towed by another fishing vessel. The casualty was towed into Lowestoft harbour and *Bernard Matthews* returned to her station. Several further services were performed during 1991, all of a routine nature. On 20 August she helped the fishing boat *Sophie Dawn*, which had a fire in her engine room, and five days later assisted the fishing vessel *Cheryl M*. On 10 October *Bernard Matthews* was launched at 3.10p.m. to the motor fishing boat *Orian*, which had broken down north-east of the Cockle Buoy. The lifeboat towed the broken down vessel to Lowestoft harbour, which was reached at 8pm. After refuelling at Gorleston, *Bernard Matthews* returned to Caister at 10.30p.m.

Soon after the new lifeboat had become operational, the station was hit by tragedy. On 1 September 1991 Coxswain Benny Read died after being fatally injured firing the maroons to call out the inshore lifeboat for what turned out to be a false alarm with good intent. The maroons exploded into his chest as he set them off. The whole village was devastated by this incident, and many messages of sympathy were received, including ones from HRH Prince Charles and HRH Princess Alexandra. Benny Read had been coxswain for more than a decade, and Second Coxswain before that. He had been a crew member at Caister for over thirty-five years, had been involved in the services to *Loch Lorgan* and *Seaforth Conqueror,* and played a major part in getting the Volunteer Rescue Service off the ground. His popularity in the village was demonstrated during his funeral when the route to the church was lined by hundreds of people as the lifeboat crew walked in front of the hearse. He was laid to rest in the Caister Parish Cemetery.

Coxswain Benny Read's gravestone. (Paul Russell)

Despite the tragic loss of Benny Read, the service carried on. A new coxswain, Richard Thurlow, was appointed, and Billy Read, Benny's younger brother, became second coxswain, continuing the Read family tradition of service to the lifeboat at Caister which stretched back more than 150 years. On 19 June 1992, they were involved in a particularly fine service. At 9.30a.m. that day, the Coastguard informed Coxswain Thurlow that the small yacht *Sea Moon* was making heavy weather off Bacton, and a few minutes later requested the launch of the lifeboat. With a gale blowing and very heavy swell on the beach, *Bernard Matthews* was taken along the beach to the south of her usual launch site where less swell made for a slightly easier and safer launch. The lifeboat was pushed into the sea on her carriage and, despite heavy seas breaking over both lifeboat and tractor, she was successfully launched. A large wave did catch the lifeboat and knock her round so she was nearly broadside on to the beach just after the launch but, using the power of her engines, the lifeboat got clear safely. The lifeboat crew found *Sea Moon* about 100 yards off Horsey Gap in heavy surf with the wind gusting to gale force 9 and an RAF air/sea rescue helicopter from Coltishall on the scene. The yacht's radio and engine had broken down, and the vessel was being kept head to sea by her sails. The yacht was being thrown violently about by the swell and attempts by the lifeboat crew to put a tow rope aboard by means of a heaving line were unsuccessful as the yacht's crew were too exhausted to make the rope fast. So it was decided to put a lifeboatman aboard the yacht. The transfer was a difficult operation due to the heavy swells, but once he was on board the yacht, he made fast the tow rope. *Bernard Matthews* was then able to pull the casualty clear of the surf and tow her into Great Yarmouth where the two yachtsmen were safely landed after their difficult ordeal.

Bernard Matthews towing the steam yacht Calola *into Lowestoft harbour in June 1994. (W.J. Keith)*

In the early hours of 9 August 1994, *Bernard Matthews* was involved in another challenging service. During the afternoon, the Coastguard contacted Coxswain Dick Thurlow with the news that the 55ft motor yacht *Smokey Bandit* had broken down three miles offshore and required help. At 3.40a.m. *Bernard Matthews* was launched and soon reached the casualty which, by this time, was firmly aground on the Scroby Sands and bumping heavily with its superstructure cracking. To reach the casualty, a passage was set which involved the lifeboat having to cross the sandbank, a difficult and dangerous task. However, this was accomplished, and the lifeboat eventually reached the yacht. The yacht's engine room was flooded as a result of the bumping on the bank, so the lifeboat was manoeuvred alongside three times in the heavy swell to take off two children and a woman. One of the lifeboatmen was left on board, with a man and two Alsatian dogs. An attempt was then made to tow the casualty clear of the sandbank. Gorleston's Atlantic 21 inshore lifeboat had by now arrived on the scene and passed a tow rope from *Bernard Matthews* to *Smokey Bandit*. Despite the heavy seas breaking on the bank, the lifeboat managed to tow the yacht clear. The yacht then started sinking despite the efforts of the lifeboatmen. Although both a portable pump and the lifeboat's own pump were being used, the volume of water was almost too great. Gorleston's all-weather lifeboat *Barham* was called out and she was able to help pump out the water while *Bernard Matthews* towed the yacht into Great Yarmouth harbour, where she was moored. However, it was not until the fire brigade arrived and deployed a large, powerful fire pump that the water in the yacht began to diminish. The vessel was then beached on the side of the river.

The Fowler tractor being used to launch Bernard Matthews *for a demonstration run in July 1995. (Nicholas Leach)*

In 1995 the Caister station celebrated the 150th anniversary of its establishment. A number of events were planned, the first of which was a civic ceremony at Great Yarmouth when the year was officially 'launched' in the presence of a number of distinguished guests, including the Lord Lieutenant of Norfolk, Sir Timothy Coleman, Bernard Matthews, as well as the Chairman of Norfolk County Council. The highlight of the year was a visit by HRH Prince Charles on 27 July 1995. This was the Prince's second visit to the station. During his tour, he cut the anniversary cake and invited all those present to toast the lifeboat. After meeting station officials and members of the crew, he was taken on a tour of the lifeboat house and boarded the lifeboat. The boat was then launched with the Prince on board and the Royal Standard hoisted on the mast. The Prince took the wheel for much of the trip and, after sailing up the river to Great Yarmouth, the lifeboat moored alongside the steam drifter *Lydia Eva* near the Town Hall. The Prince then departed with another large crowd in attendance.

During the autumn of that year, *Bernard Matthews* performed two fine rescues within the space of a week. The first took place on 24 September after Great Yarmouth Coastguard had received a message from the Norwegian roll-on roll-off ferry *Aurora* that the 48ft Dutch yacht *Madame* was in difficulties to the east of the Smiths Knoll light float, approximately twenty-five miles from Caister. *Bernard Matthews* was launched at 3.40p.m. and set course through a gap in the Scroby Sands to the position of the casualty. Conditions at the scene were bad with a north-westerly wind and 10ft to 15ft swell so *Aurora* attempted to give the yacht a lee. The lifeboat arrived on the scene at 5p.m. and found the yacht's jib loose and ropes hanging over the side. It was soon apparent that the nine-man crew of the

Bernard Matthews *entering Great Yarmouth harbour in 1995 with the bishop of Great Yarmouth on board.* *(Nicholas Leach)*

RNLI Director Brian Miles and his wife visited Caister in 1995 as part of the station's 150th anniversary celebrations. He was presented with a framed picture of the lifeboat Bernard Matthews. *(Ivor Steadman)*

Prince Charles, escorted by Coxswain Richard Thurlow, meets the families and friends associated with Caister VRS in July 1995 during the station's 150th anniversary celebrations. (Ivor Steadman)

yacht were exhausted and unable to cope with the situation through severe sea sickness. One of the Caister lifeboatmen was put aboard to assist as *Madame* was pitching about erratically. The yacht's bilges were full of water and diesel fuel and none of its crew was able to assist in connecting the tow. A second lifeboatman was therefore put on board and, with great difficulty, a tow was connected. *Bernard Matthews* with *Madame* in tow, then made for Great Yarmouth harbour in conditions which were very uncomfortable for both boats. During the course of the tow, one sea hit the lifeboat and put out the starboard navigation light, while the yacht's foresail was carried away and the main boom broke from the mast. The two vessels reached the relative safety of Yarmouth Roads and at 9.30p.m. entered Great Yarmouth harbour where the nine young people were safely landed. For this service, an award was received from the Royal Netherlands Lifeboat Service.

The second rescue took place on 1 October 1995. In a force 5-6 wind, with a misty rain falling, *Bernard Matthews* was launched at 4.50a.m., under the command of Coxswain Dick Thurlow, to the yacht *Sequina*. A northerly gale in the North Sea two days before had continued to cause a heavy swell on the Scroby Sands. A red parachute flare, followed by a red hand-held flare, had been sighted from the beach. As the lifeboat proceeded to the casualty, radio contact with it was established. The operator on board the casualty said their boat was listing and taking in water, and it subsequently capsized. Before radio contact was lost, however, the crew of the yacht were advised to try to stay with their upturned vessel. As the lifeboat crossed the sandbank in complete darkness the lifeboat's searchlights were used to look for people who might be in the water. With little depth of water in which to manoeuvre, the lifeboat was being bounced on the sands.

Sequina was seen through the spray lying on her side, having been knocked onto the bank by the swell and the south-east force 7 wind, which had moderated to force 5-6 by the time the lifeboat arrived. *Sequina* was lying with her bow facing south with a

The Fowler tractor built in 1954 by the RNLI as T62. It served as a lifeboat launching vehicle at Bridlington, Scarborough, Runswick, Sheringham and Ilfracombe, before being sold to the Caister VRS in 1989. She served at Caister as T2 until 1996. (David Gooch)

Bernard Matthews *leaves Great Yarmouth harbour at speed. (Nicholas Leach)*

Recovery of Bernard Matthews *on the beach at Caister, being hauled out of the water over skids prior to being pulled onto her carriage using the tractor's winch. (Nicholas Leach)*

seventy-five degree list. Her boom was sticking into the sand and had prevented the vessel totally capsizing. The crew, two men and two women, were standing on the starboard rail in the cockpit and the sea was breaking over the yacht. A strong ebb tide and sweep were running past the vessel. Coxswain Thurlow attempted to get the lifeboat close to the wreck three times but each time she was swept away. On the fourth attempt, the coxswain rammed the lifeboat into the wreck and the lifeboat crew succeeded in pulling the survivors off the casualty and into the lifeboat. The lifeboat was held in position throughout by the power of her engines. Once the survivors had been brought to safety, the lifeboat was driven clear of the wreck and, with even less water on the bank, headed into the swatchway. She then made for Great Yarmouth and was moored at the quay where the survivors were landed, one of whom was taken to hospital suffering from hypothermia. These two fine services were formally recognised by the RNLI. At a ceremony held on 24 June 1996 at Great Yarmouth Town Hall, District Inspector Richard Perks presented the station as a whole with a Letter of Thanks, received on behalf of the station by Coxswain Thurlow.

In 1996 a new launching tractor, funded partly by a donation of £50,000 from Bernard Matthews, was bought for the station. During August that year, a series of launching and recovery trials with the lifeboat were held to test out a Caterpillar 75C type tractor (registration number K418 TFE). This design of tractor, weighing seventeen tons and powered by a 300hp engine, is used in the Netherlands by the KNRM (Royal Dutch lifeboat Society) for launching lifeboats across the flat beaches typical of that country. In

Bernard Matthews presents the crew with a cheque for £50,000 towards the new launching tractor in December 1996, handing over the cheque to Coxswain Richard Thurlow. (Ivor Steadman)

December 1996, following the success of the trials, an order was placed for the new tractor and an appeal launched to raise the £150,000 needed. The new vehicle arrived the following year and is now in service with the CVRS.

In 1999, another sad loss overtook the station with the death of John 'Skipper' Woodhouse, described as a 'Caister legend' and famous throughout the country for his appearances on national television during the early 1990s when the new lifeboat appeal was in full swing. Skipper, as he was known to all, had a special place in the history of the station, and so deserves a special mention as he is fondly remembered by all connected with Caister lifeboat. He saw lifeboat work as his duty and explained: 'There was never any option. We were longshore fishermen and it was tradition they formed the crew of the lifeboat. It was as simple as that.' Although he first crewed the lifeboat in 1933, at a time when not only his father but also his grandfather were in the crew, his involvement with the service went back before that. As a boy he used to run round the village and help gather the crew when they were needed and in 1927 was officially enrolled as a shore helper. The station mechanic from 1941 until 1969, he received the MBE in 1993 in recognition of his services to the station. When the Caister Volunteer Rescue Service was established in 1969, he became heavily involved in its running and ensured the station remained operational after the RNLI's withdrawal. Although his health prevented him from going to sea after the mid-1970s, he carried on as a shore helper and kept a record of every launch that was undertaken by the lifeboat. He died in the early hours of 17 October 1999, aged eighty-six.

Launching Bernard Matthews *with the Caterpillar tractor in 1987. (From a postcard in the author's collection)*

Recovery of Bernard Matthews *using the Caterpillar tractor specially adapted for launching the lifeboat. (Paul Durrant)*

'Skipper' Woodhouse at Caister during lifeboat day in August 1994. (Ivor Steadman)

The day after Skipper's death, 18 October 1999, *Bernard Matthews* was needed for a difficult and arduous service. She was launched at 10.37p.m. into a heavy swell with a force 7 wind to go to the help of the Lithuanian yacht *Barracuda*, which had six persons on board. The lifeboat, under the command of Coxswain Richard Thurlow, found the yacht aground on the North Scroby Buoy being thrown around by a heavy breaking sea. The lifeboat was brought close to the yacht three times in an attempt to secure a towline, sustaining some damage to the handrails in the process. Once the tow line was secured, the lifeboat pulled the yacht away from the sandbank into deeper water and began towing it to Great Yarmouth. As the general sea state was so bad, and the risk of the yacht capsizing quite high, the Gorleston all-weather lifeboat *Samarbeta* was launched and arrived at 11.27p.m. to provide an escort. Crossing the bar at the entrance to Great Yarmouth harbour proved somewhat hazardous, but once this was accomplished, the casualty was safely moored at the Seamen's Mission at 12.14a.m. on 19 October. Because of the conditions, *Bernard Matthews* remained at Great Yarmouth overnight and returned to her station the following day.

During 1999, much-needed improvements to the station's shore facilities were started. The lifeboat house, designed by Posford Duvivier for the RNLI, had been built in 1941 for the station's first motor lifeboat by Messrs Chaston, a local builder. It had replaced a smaller building situated to the south which had been used as a gear store, and which was later moved when in private ownership. The improvements involved the construction of a new extension which incorporated a meeting and training room, a

Bernard Matthews *returning in March 2000 from a short refit at Goodchild Marine. (Peter Edey)*

Caterpillar tractor T4 hauls Bernard Matthews *out of the water for recovery on 17 March 2000. (Peter Edey)*

The lifeboat house seen in February 1999 during the extensive rebuilding undertaken to improve the station's facilities. (Nicholas Leach)

workshop, and increased space for a new and larger lifeboat, thus bringing a new dimension to the operation of the station. The building was funded by a bequest from William Thomas Spencer of Caystreward, Great Yarmouth, a former officer in the Merchant Navy. It was designed by Fordham & Johns, of Regent Street, Great Yarmouth, and construction work was carried out by M. S. Oakes Ltd, of Mobbs Way, Lowestoft, at a cost of £210,000.

The extension to the lifeboat house was formally opened in the presence of HRH Princess Alexandra at a ceremony held at Caister on Saturday 6 May 2000. This marked another milestone in the history of the Caister Volunteer Rescue Service. As well as the opening of the boathouse extension, a memorial plaque was unveiled to the late John 'Skipper' Woodhouse. On arriving at Caister, Princess Alexandra was greeted by John Sheppard, Chairman of Norfolk County Council, Jack Barnes, Chairman of Great Yarmouth Borough Council, Harry Barker, Chairman of the CVRS, and Geoffrey Freeman, Vice-Chairman of CVRS. She was then taken to the lifeboat house, toured the new facilities and introduced to the lifeboat crew. There followed a private meeting with the Friends and Supporters of CVRS in the crew meeting room, where a short dedication was conducted by the Revd Tim Thomson, Rector of Caister and a director of CVRS, after which both lifeboats were launched for a short demonstration.

In the first year of the new Millennium, Caister lifeboat continued to prove her worth. On 11 July 2000, she was launched to assist the Cromer all-weather lifeboat *Ruby and Arthur Reed II* tow the Lowestoft-based historic sailing smack *Excelsior* and her nine-person crew to safety during stormy seas. The smack's giant tiller had snapped in two during gale force winds, and the vessel soon got into difficulty in the heavy weather. Despite rigging temporary steering and managing to get clear of the sands, help was still

The lifeboat house in 2001 after the completion of the extension and internal refurbishment. (Nicholas Leach)

required. Cromer lifeboat was launched to her shortly after 10.30p.m., but had difficulty keeping up with the stricken vessel as it was travelling at high speed in the strong winds, and so *Bernard Matthews* was called to assist. During the rescue, Cromer lifeboat was buffeted by 20ft waves and lost some of her electronic navigation equipment. However, the lifeboatmen managed to attach a towrope to the smack and, with Caister lifeboat acting a navigator, the three vessels arrived in Lowestoft harbour at about 4a.m. According to Coxswain Dick Thurlow, the conditions were among the worst he had ever experienced during summer months: 'The weather was getting worse and worse and by the time we decided to assist it was up to around gale force 9. They were exceptionally bad conditions for this time of year. The crew were very lucky but they did an excellent job managing to keep things together for so long without any proper steering equipment.' *Bernard Matthews* returned to her station in the early hours of 12 July after another fine service performed by the lifeboat men and women of Caister. During 2001, the station remembered those who had given their lives in serving the Caister lifeboat.

Appendix 1
Lifeboats

ON	Name Donor	Dimensions Type/Built	Years on station	Launches/ lives saved
Pre-RNLI lifeboats				
–	Unnamed	NSR	1829-43	unknown
–	Unnamed	29ft 6in x 11ft 6in NSR	1845-46	unknown
–	Unnamed County Subscriptions	42ft x 11ft 6in N&S/1846	1846-65★	(1957-65) 23/133

★ Taken over by RNLI in 1857; life-saving record dates from RNLI takeover

ON	Name Donor	Dimensions Type/Built	Years on station	Launches/ lives saved
No.1 Station				
–	*James Pearce,* *Birmingham No.2* Birmingham Lifeboat Fund renamed *Covent Garden* in 1878 appropriated to Covent Garden LB Fund	42ft x 11ft 10in N&S/1865	1865-83	135/484
17	*Covent Garden* Covent Garden Lifeboat Fund	42ft x 11ft 6in N&S/1883	1883-99	55/208
431	*Covent Garden* Covent Garden Lifeboat Fund	40ft x 12ft N&S/1899	1899-1919	153/166
607	*James Leath* Legacy of James Leath, London	42ft x 12ft 6in N&S/1910	1919-29	23/18
No.2 Station				
18	*The Boys* Routledge's *Magazine for Boys* renamed *Godsend* in 1875	32ft 6in x 10ft N&S/1867	1867-92	128/410

327	*Beauchamp* Sir R. Proctor-Beauchamp Bt, Norwich	36ft x 10ft 6in N&S/1892	1892-1901	84/146
506	*Nancy Lucy* Sir Henry W. Lucy, MP, London	35ft x 10ft 9in N&S/1903	1903-29	42/144
526	*Charles Burton* Legacy of Charles T.H. Burton	38ft x 10ft 9in Liverpool/1904	1929-41	31/15
834	*Jose Neville* Mrs E. Neville, Barnes, Surrey	35ft 6in x 10ft 3in Liverpool motor/1941	1941-64	107/75
978	*The Royal Thames* Legacy of Mr Forster, gifts from Miss Ellison and Mr G.J.F. Jackson, as well as RNLI funds.	37ft x 11ft 6in Oakley/1964	1964-69	30/15

Volunteer Rescue Service

(906)	*Shirley Jean Adye* BP Great Yarmouth and local fund-raising	35ft 6in x 10ft 8in Liverpool motor/1953	1973-91	88/55
–	*Bernard Matthews* Bernard Matthews and local fund-raising	38ft 6in x 13ft Lochlin/1991	1991-	

Years on station	1846-Oct 1865
Record	23 launches, 133 lives saved
	(from 1857 when RNLI took over station)
Donor	Norfolk Shipwreck Association
Type	Norfolk & Suffolk
Year	built 1846
Builder	Branford, Great Yarmouth
Dimensions	Length 42ft, breadth 11ft 6in
Notes	Taken over by the RNLI in 1857
Disposal	Condemned and sold 1865

James Pearce, Birmingham No.2/Covent Garden

Years on station	Oct 1865-1883
Record	135 launches, 484 lives saved
Donor	Birmingham Lifeboat Fund; appropriated to the Covent Garden Lifeboat Fund in 1878.
Naming Ceremony	Named at Great Yarmouth on 25 October 1865 by Miss Steward, daughter of the Mayor.
Type	Norfolk & Suffolk
Year built	1865
Builder	Mills & Blake, Great Yarmouth
Dimensions	Length 42ft, breadth 11ft 10in
Disposal	Condemned 1883

The Boys/Godsend

Years on station	No.2 lifeboat, Sept 1867-21 Jan 1892
Record	125 launches, 410 lives saved
Donor	Gift of Routledge's Magazine for Boys, through collection by Edmund Routledge, Editor; renamed *Godsend* in 1875 after being appropriated to the gift of Lady Bourchier, Hampton Court Palace
Naming Ceremony	10 September 1867
Cost	£152 9s 4d
Official Number	18
Type	Norfolk & Suffolk
Year built	1867
Builder	Beeching, Great Yarmouth
Dimensions	Length 32ft 6in, breadth 10ft, twelve oars
Disposal	Sold

Covent Garden

Years on station	No.1 lifeboat, 1 Nov 1883 – 5 Dec 1899
Official Number	17
Record	55 launches, 208 lives saved
Donor	Covent Garden Lifeboat Fund.
Naming ceremony	3 November 1883 at Great Yarmouth
Cost	£300
Type	Norfolk & Suffolk
Year built	1883
Builder	Beeching, Gt Yarmouth
Dimensions	Length 42ft, breadth 11ft 6in, depth 3ft 11in
Disposal	Broken up January 1900

Beauchamp

Years on station	No.2 lifeboat, January 1892-1901
Record	84 launches, 146 lives saved
Donor	Gift of Sir R. Proctor-Beauchamp, Bt, Norwich
Naming ceremony	21 January 1892, christened by Lady Violet Proctor-Beauchamp
Cost	£266 3s 9d
Official Number	327
Type	Norfolk & Suffolk, twelve-oared
Year built	1892
Builder	J.H. Critten, Great Yarmouth
Dimensions	Length 36ft, breadth 10ft 6in, depth 3ft 11in
Disposal	Wrecked on service 1901, sold locally September 1902; later broken up.

Covent Garden

Years on station	No.1 lifeboat, 5 December 1899–1919
Record	153 launches, 166 lives saved
Donor	Covent Garden Lifeboat Fund
Cost	£1,295 7s 5d
Official Number	431
Type	Norfolk & Suffolk, twelve-oared
Year built	1899
Builder	Thames Iron Works, Blackwall, London
Dimensions	Length 40ft, breadth 12ft, depth 4ft 5in
Disposal	Condemned and broken up January 1920

Years on station	No.2 lifeboat, 12 June – 1903 November 1929
Record	42 launches, 144 lives saved
Donor	Gift of Sir Henry W. Lucy, MP, London
Naming ceremony	Named 23 July 1903 by the Countess of Selbourne
Cost	£1,603 9s 8d
Official Number	506
Type	Norfolk & Suffolk, 'improved' type, twelve-oared
Year built	1903
Builder	Thames Iron Works, Blackwall, London; yard no.TK27
Dimensions	Length 35ft, breadth 10ft 9in, depth 4ft 5in
Weight	6tons 10cwt 1qtr
Notes	On the stern of the boat was inscribed on a blue ribband in gold letters, the phrase 'Caister men never turn back'.
Disposal	Sold 1929 for £52 10s and converted into a houseboat at Norwich; current whereabouts unknown.

Years on station	No.1 lifeboat, November 1919 – November 1929
Record	23 launches, 18 lives saved
Donor	Legacy of James Leath, London.
Cost	£1,933 16s 3d
Official Number	607
Type	Norfolk & Suffolk
Year built	1910
Builder	Thames Iron Works, Blackwall, London; yard no.TL52
Dimensions	Length 42ft, breadth 12ft 6in, breadth 4ft 8in
Notes	Served at Pakefield 1910-19, later
Disposal	Sold 15 August 1935 for £65 and converted into a houseboat based at Poole; subsequently obtained for display at Chatham Historic Dockyard.

Years on station	November 1929 – May 1941
Record	31 launches, 15 lives saved
Donor	Legacy of Charles T H Burton.
Cost	£1,044
Official Number	526

Type	Liverpool
Year built	1904
Builder	Thames Iron Works, Blackwall, London
Dimensions	Length 38ft, breadth 10ft 9in, depth 4ft 4in
Notes	Originally stationed at Grimsby, where she served 1904-27
Disposal	Sold February 1942, became the fishing boat *Silver Queen*; current whereabouts unknown

Jose-Neville

Years on station	May 1941 – February 1964
Record	107 launches, 75 lives saved
Donor	Legacy of Mrs Ellen Neville, Barnes, Surrey
Cost	£4,473 15s 11d
Official Number	834
Type	Liverpool motor
Year built	1941
Builder	Groves & Guttridge, Cowes, Isle of Wight
Dimensions	Length 35ft 6in, breadth 10ft 3in
Engines	Single 35hp Weyburn AE six-cylinder petrol
Disposal	Sold August 1966, became the fishing boat *Concorde* LT267 operating out of Southwold; later moved to Slaughden Quay where a new whaleback cabin was added.

The Royal Thames

Years on station	February 1964 – 17 October 1969
Record	30 launches, 15 lives saved
Donor	Legacy of Mr D.A. Forster, gifts from Mr G.J.F. Jackson and Miss Gwladys Ellison; and RNLI funds.
Naming Ceremony	Named on 14 July 1964 by the Hon. Mrs Valentine Wyndham-Quin.
Cost	£31,749
Official Number	978
Type	Oakley
Year built	1964
Builder	J. Samuel White, East Cowes, Isle of Wight
Dimensions	Length 37ft, breadth 11ft 6in
Engines	Twin 52hp Parsons Porbeagle four-cylinder diesels
Notes	After Caister, transferred to Runswick 1970-78, then Pwllheli 1979-91 and finally Clogher Head 1991-93
Disposal	Scrapped 1994

A fine photograph of The Royal Thames *in August 1969 which shows the deck layout of the 37ft Oakley class. When built, lifeboats of the class, such as* The Royal Thames, *had an open aft cockpit and were not fitted with radar. Both of these features were modified as the boats continued in service. (Eastern Counties Newspapers)*

Shirley Jean Adye

Years on station	August 1973 – May 1991
Record	88 launches, 57 lives saved
Donor	Legacy of Mr William Ross MacArthur, Glasgow.
Naming ceremony	21 July 1953 at St Abbs, christened *W. Ross MacArthur* of Glasgow by Mrs Sommerville, wife of Mr A. Sommerville of Glasgow, who had presented the boat to the RNLI. Christened *Shirley Jean Adye* at Caister on 5 August 1973 by Mrs Shirley Adye.
Cost	£4,500 (£14,398 when new)
Official Number	906
Type	Liverpool motor
Year built	1953
Builder	Groves & Guttridge, Cowes, Isle of Wight
Dimensions	Length 35ft 6in, breadth 10ft 8in
Engines	Twin 20hp Ferry Kadency FKR.3 three-cylinder diesels/ 1987- twin 51bhp Perkins 4108 diesels, with Borg Warner Velvet drive 2:1 reduction hydraulic gearboxes.

Recovery of Shirley Jean Adye *on the beach. This photograph shows the tunnels in which the propellers were located, and the rudder in its retracted position. The radar on the engine casing was fitted after the RNLI sold the lifeboat out of service. (Paul Russell)*

Notes	Originally operated by the RNLI, served at St Abbs 1953-64, then sold in 1968
Disposal	Sold to Pembroke Dock Authority in July 1992, renamed *Mariners Friend*; sold again in October 1994, bought by Alan Baker, of Sutton Coldfield, and taken to Bassetts Pole, near Sutton.

Bernard Matthews

Years on station	May 1991 to date
Donor	Local Appeal and generous donation by Bernard Matthews.
Naming ceremony	18 June 1991, christened by HRH Princess Alexandra.
Cost	Approximately £400,000
Operational Number	38-01
Type	Lochin
Year built	1990
Builder	Lochin Marine, Rye; fitted out by Goodchild Marine Services, Burgh Castle, Great Yarmouth
Dimensions	Length 38ft 6in, breadth 10ft 8in
Engines	Twin 282hp Ford Sabre diesels, speed 18 knots

The Volunteer Rescue Service's purpose-built lifeboat, 38ft Lochin Bernard Matthews. (From a postcard in the author's collection)

First inshore-lifeboat

Years on station   1970-c.1975
Donor   Bought by local school children.

Second inshore lifeboat

Years on station   1972-1991
Donor   CVRS funds

Inshore Lifeboat Jim Davidson

Years on station   1991-2001
Donor   Funded by end of the pier show at Great Yarmouth

Years on station	April 2001 to date
Type	Searider SR4.7M high speed rescue craft
Hull	Rigid hull inflatable with reinforced inflatable buoyancy collar, in orange
Engine	60hp Mercury outboard, two-stroke oil injection, twelve gallons petrol
Equipment	Blue light, VHF radio, centre console steering
Capability	Night time launch subject to weather, fitted with navigation lights

After Service

What became of the lifeboats after their service at Caister had ended? *Jose Neville* and *Shirley Jean Adye* are now in private hands and can be seen in Suffolk and Cornwall respectively. *The Royal Thames* is out of the water at Hewitts Yard, Blakeney, Norfolk. The whereabouts of most of the sailing lifeboats is unknown, although *James Leath* can be seen on display at Chatham Historic Dockyard as part of the National Lifeboat Collection.

The latest addition to Caister's life-saving equiptment is the Avon rigid-inflatable Jim Davidson MBE, seen on Caister beach on 21 June 2001. (Gary Markham)

After service at Caister Shirley Jean Adye *was sold to Darrel Davies, of Tenby, in July 1992. She was renamed* Mariners Friend, *but was sold again, in October 1994, to Alan Baker of Bassets Pole, Sutton Coldfield. She was taken to Bassets Pole, where she spent several years before being moved to Falmouth Marina by road. She is now kept at Falmouth Bt Co., Flushing. The photograph shows her at Bassets Pole with her owner, Alan Baker.*

Jose Neville, *after service at Caister, was sold out of RNLI service in 1966 and became a pilot boat for the Lowestoft pilots. Towards the end of 1972, she was sold to became a fishing boat operating out of Southwold and Walberswick and renamed* Concorde. *She had a wheelhouse added during her time as a fishing boat. During the early 1990s she was obtained by the current owners, who had a whaleback cabin added and used her as a fishing boat at Slaughden Quay, near Aldeburgh. Shown here undergoing refurbishment at Slaughden Quay in February 1998. (Nicholas Leach)*

Appendix 2
Service Summary

The Caister lifeboats have performed hundreds of rescues and saved many lives. In 1955 it was stated that the Caister lifeboat station had saved 1,752 lives, more then any other, while the Ramsgate lifeboats had saved 1,662 lives, and Great Yarmouth and Gorleston lifeboats 1,748 lives. These figures show just how busy the Caister lifeboats were, particularly in the nineteenth century, when at some stations it was not unusual for there to be several years between service calls. Although more recently, and especially since the introduction of inshore lifeboats, it is not uncommon for some stations to undertake more than 100 rescues a year, few stations were as busy as Caister during the ninenteenth century.

Early Rescues

1852	Dec 17	Schooner *Paulina*, of Dartmouth, assisted to save vessel and	7
	26-7	Brig *Agnes*, saved vessel and crew and saved Brig *Active*, saved crew	13
1853	Feb 23	Sloop *Hannah*, of Gainsborough, saved vessel	
1855	Jan 30	Brig *Stranger*, of North Shields, saved	1

Lifeboat of 1858

1858	Dec 18	Brig *Prophete*, of London, saved	11
1861	Jan 6	Brig *Arethusa*, of Blyth, saved	8
	Nov 14	Brig *Lively*, of Clay, assisted to save vessel and	5
1862	Feb 26	Brig Sisters, of Whitby, saved	9
	May 4	Schooner *Trial*, of Poole, saved	7
	Oct 19-20	Schooner *Hannah Booth*, of Plymouth, saved derelict vessel	
1863	Jan 15	Schooner *Kezia*, of Sunderland, saved	5
	22	Schooner *Emily*, of London, assisted to save vessel	
1864	Oct 17-9	Steamship *Ontario*, of Liverpool, assisted in salvage operations	
	19	do., in two trips, transferred 55 labourers to tugs	
1865	Oct 1	Brig *Nautilus*, of South Shields, saved	9
	4	Brig *Harlington*, of Sunderland, saved	9
	9	Brig *Kathleen*, of Hartlepool, saved vessel	
	10	do., landed 3 from a light-vessel	

James Pearce, Birmingham No.2

1865	Oct 25	Schooner *Maria*, of Hull, saved vessel	
	Nov 8	Brig *Raven*, of London, saved vessel and	10
	Dec 11	Brig *Lucy*, of Sunderland, saved vessel and	6
1866	Jan 18	Brig *Tartar*, of Sunderland, saved vessel and	8
	20	Brigantine *George*, of Goole, assisted to save vessel	
	Feb 16	Steamship *Lady Beatrix*, of Sunderland, saved vessel	
	April 7	Steamship *Corbon*, of Newcastle, assisted to save vessel and	12
	Nov 30	Schooner *Coronation*, of London, saved	8
	Dec 28	Brig *Kelpie*, of London, saved vessel and	8
1867	Jan 16	Schooner *Clyde*, of Yarmouth, saved	5
	Feb 8	Sloop *Telegraph*, of Sunderland, saved	3
	28	Fishing smack *Striver*, of Yarmouth, saved smack and	5
	Mar 7	Schooner *Louise*, saved vessel and	7
	May 21	Schooner *New Whim*, of Portsmouth, saved	3
		Brig *William and Sarah*, of South Shields, saved vessel	
		Brig *Union*, Cowes, landed	7
	Oct 27	Newarp Light-vessel, rendered assistance	
	Nov 18	Schooner *Polydesa*, saved vesse	1
1868	Feb 23	Ship *Omega*, of Newcastle, saved	7
	Mar 8	Barque *Sparkling Wave*, of Sunderland, saved (also a dog)	15
	28	Schooner *Wave*, of Boston, saved vessel and	4
	May 23-4	Barque *Balder*, of Sweden, assisted to save vessel	
	Oct 23-6	Steamship *Ganges*, of Hull, stood by and assisted to save vessel	
	Nov 30	Barque *Annie Scott*, of Arbroath, saved	9
	Dec 22	Schooner *Pioneer*, of Exeter, saved	4
	28	Brig *Bilboa*, of Seaham, saved	6
1869	Jan 3	A foreign vessel, stood by	
		Brig *Elizabeth*, of Blyth, saved	6
	Feb 15	Barque *Eliza Caroline*, of London, rendered assistance	
	22	Ship *Hannah Petterson*, of Bergen, saved	20
	Apr 29	Steamship *Lady Flora*, of Hull, stood by	
	Oct 28	Barque *Alma*, of Malta, rendered assistance	
	Dec 1	Barque *Helsingoe*, of Elsinore, saved	14
1870	Dec 5	Brig *Boune Castle*, of Whitby, assisted to save vessel	
	9	Brig *Wamderer*, of Whitby, assisted to save vesse	1
1871	Feb 22	Barque *Jane Kilgour*, of London, saved	13
	Sep 24	Schooner *Angola*, of Beaumaris, assisted to save vessel	
		Sloop *Trafalgar*, of Cley, saved vessel and	2
	Oct 31	Brigantine *Norval*, of Sunderland, assisted to save vessel	
	Nov 14-5	Steamship *Benjamin Whitworth*, of Middlesborough, assisted to save vessel	
1872	Oct 10	Brig *Eglantine*, of Whitby, assisted to save vessel	
	18	Ship *St Johanner*, of Danzig, assisted to save vessel and	18
	Nov 5	Schooner *Mary Grace*, of Whitstable, assisted to save vessel and	7
1873	Jan 6	Steamship *Druid*, of Sunderland, landed	5
	Oct 20	Brig *Hendon*, of Sunderland, assisted to save vessel and	9
1874	Dec 13	Unknown vessel, rendered assistance	
1875	Jan 29	Ship *Oriental*, of North Shields, assisted to save vessel	
	Mar 4	Ship *China*, of South Shields, assisted to save vessel and	22
	Oct 21	Barque *Young England*, of Middlesborough, saved	4

	Nov 3	Brigantine *Harmston*, of Newcastle, saved	7
1876	Mar 19	Schooner *Killin*, of Greenock, saved	5
	June 10	Ship *McNear*, of Boston (USA), assisted to save vessel	
1878	Mar 28	Barque *Theresa*, of North Shields, saved	11
		Brig *Wladiener*, of Libau, saved	8

The same lifeboat renamed *Covent Garden*

1878	Nov 6	Fishing smack *Mystery*, of Great Yarmouth, assisted to save smack	
	14	Boat of schooner *F. Edwards*, of Grimsby, saved	5
	Dec 30	Barque *Palmyra*, of South Shields, assisted to save vessel	
1879	Mar 25	Brig *Cito*, of Arendal, saved	7
	26	do., assisted to beach wrecked vessel	
	Nov 12	Brig *Latvia*, of Guernsey, assisted to save vessel	
	Dec 28	Brig *Rival*, of Blyth, saved	8
		1880 Jan 2 Steamship *Amcott*, of West Hartlepool, assisted to save vessel	
	Nov 1	Fishing smack *Iron Duke*, of London, assisted to save smack and	6
	6	Steamship *Swan*, of Liverpool, assisted to save vessel	
	16	Steamship *Ringdove*, of Liverpool, saved	16
1881	March 5	Barque *Angostura*, of Hamburg, assisted to save vessel and	17
	Aug 25	Barque *Strathdon*, of Dundee, saved	12
	Nov 16	Fishing dandy *Scud*, of Yarmouth, saved	6
1882	Mar 7	Barque *Canmore*, of Dundee, assisted to save vessel and	17
	Apr 15	Steamship *Consent*, of Sunderland, rendered assistance	
	June 1	Brig *Aigle*, of St Servan, saved	6
	Sep 13	Dandy *Reine des Agnes*, of Boulogne, landed 8 from a steamship	
	Dec 17	Steamship *Bradley*, of Liverpool, assisted to save vessel and	15
1883	Jan 26	Brigantine *Dare*, of Sunderland, assisted to save vessel and	6
	Sep 19	Steamship *Isis*, of Newcastle, rendered assistance	
	Oct 20	Barque *Arab*, of Apenrade, assisted to save vessel and	15

Covent Garden (second)

1883	Nov 18	Barge *Garson*, of Wisbech, saved	4
	Dec 7	Barque *Zelos*, of Grimstad, assisted to save vessel and	10
	17	Brig *Clara*, of Dublin, assisted to save vessel and	7
1884	Jan 30	Schooner *Sarnian Gem*, of Guernsey, rendered assistance	
	Feb 1	Schooner *Mizpah*, of Dover, stood by	
	Oct 7	Steamship *Speedwell*, of Hull, saved	14
	Dec 5	Schooner *Annie*, of Wick, assisted to save vessel and	5
	29	Barque *Lorely*, of Arendal, assisted to save vessel and	12
1885	Mar 8	Three-masted schooner AKYAB, of Genoa, assisted to save vessel and	11
	9-10	Steamship *Beale*, of Scarborough, saved (also a dog)	20
		do., (second service) assisted to save vessel	
1886	Jan 18	Schooner *Syren*, landed 6 from Cockle light-vessel	
	Dec 16	Steamship *Ben Macdui*, of Aberdeen, assisted to save vessel and	12
1888	Jan 10-2	Steamship *Lady Anne*, of Sunderland, assisted to save vessel	
	Mar 15	Ship *Andromeda*, of Geestemunde, saved	16
	Nov 5	Barque *Vauban*, of Havre, saved	15
1890	Apr 19	Boat of dandy *Boy Ernest*, of Great Yarmouth, saved	6

	Oct 29-30	Four-masted ship *Nile*, of Glasgow, rendered assistance	
	Nov 19	Steamship *Carthagena*, of London, stood by	
1891	May 14	Steamship *Cambria*, of Dundee, saved	9
1894	Feb 9-11	Steamship *Resolven*, of Cardiff, saved 46 labourers, 21 crew, also 3 pigs, 3 dogs	= 67
1896	Feb 23	Barque *Glenbervie*, of Glasgow, rendered assistance	

Covent Garden (third)

1901	Jan 2	Schooner *Bertha*, of Yarmouth, assisted to save vessel	
1902	Aug 10	Steamship *Araucania*, of Liverpool, landed 6 and stood by	
	Oct 28	Dandy *Admiral*, of Lowestoft, saved (also dog and cat)	9
1903	Jan 19	Steamship *Fenham*, of Sunderland, assisted to save vessel	
	Feb 15	Ketch *Evelyn*, of Jersey, rendered assistance	
	21	Steamship *Martello*, of Hull, landed	31
1904	Jan 17	Schooner *Jasper*, of Fowey, landed 4 and a body from Newarp light-vessel	
1905	Jan 21	Ship *Jessomene*, of Liverpool, rendered assistance	
	Dec 27	Steamship *Rockliff*, of West Hartlepool, rendered assistance	
1906	Jan 5	Steamship *Harriet*, of Middlesborough, assisted to save vessel	
	31	Steamship *Newburn*, of Newcastle, stood by	
	Mar 7	Brigantine *Lady Constance*, of West Hartlepool, stood by	
1907	Jan 24	Dandy *Successor*, of Lowestoft, stood by	
	Feb 15	Dandy *Francis Roberts*, of Lowestoft, saved vessel and	5
	May 20	HMS *Cherwell*, rendered assistance	
		HMS *Ettrick*, rendered assistance	
1908	Dec 10	Barge *Ernest Piper*, of London, saved vessel (No.1 crew also saved 3 lives by lines from the shore)	
1909	Jan 17	Brigantine *Thirza*, of Whitstable, assisted to save vessel and	7
	Apr 25	Steamship *North Gwalia*, of London, landed 16 from a light-vessel	
		Steamship *Mauranger*, of Bergen, reboarded 5 of crew	
	June 16	Steamship *Kossuth Ferencz*, of Fiume, stood by	
	Sep 21	Brigantine *Parthenia*, of Yarmouth, saved (also a dog)	6
1910	Jan 5	Steamship *Orkla*, of Leith, assisted to save vessel	
	Sep 4	Barge *Empress of India*, of Ipswich, saved	4
	Oct 21	Barque *Ceres*, of Krageroe, saved	10
	30	Steamship *Claudia*, of Stockton, assisted to save vessel and	30
	Nov 28	Steamship *Edie*, of Goole, rendered assistance	
	Dec 15	Schooner *Elizabeth Bennett*, of Liverpool, stood by	
1912	Jan 11	Schooner *Falke*, of Bremen, saved	7
	13	Steamship *Glenside*, of Newcastle, stood by	
	18	Steamship *Altyre*, of Aberdeen, assisted to save vessel and	16
	21	Steam trawler *Apollo*, of Sandefjord, saved vessel	
	Dec 11-2	Steamship *Nottingham*, of Grimsby, assisted to save vessel	
1913	Jan 26	Brigantine *Wilma*, of Bremerhaven, assisted to save vessel	
	Feb 23	Schooner *Advance*, of Plymouth, saved	5
	Aug 10	Steamship *Wrexham*, of Grimsby, stood by	
	Sep 26	Steam drifter *Boadicea*, of Great Yarmouth, saved vessel and	10
	Oct 29	Steam drifter *Emerald*, of Lowestoft, saved	8
1914	Nov 9	Admiralty Minesweeper *Muckland*, rendered assistance	
1915	Mar 18-20	Steamship *Buccaneer*, of West Hartlepool, assisted to save vessel	
	July 23	Fishing smack *John and Emma*, of Lowestoft, stood by	

	Dec 5-6	Steamship *Inger Johanne*, of Bergen, saved	9
1916	Jan 15	Steamship *Derereux*, of London, stood by	
	Sep 13	HM Patrol boat, stood by	
1917	Mar 16	HM Submarine, stood by and assisted vessel	
	Apr 13	Smack *Successful*, of Lowestoft, stood by	
	May 27	Schooner *Surprise*, of Arbroath, assisted to save derelict vessel	
	Aug 29	Steamship *Lunbetty*, of London, stood by	
	Nov 26-7	Steamship *Watchland*, of West Hartlepool, assisted to save vessel and	14
1918	Dec 10	Steamship *Oakford*, of Dublin, rendered assistance	
		Steamship *Onsala*, stood by	
1919	Jan 9	Steamship *Buffs*, of London, stood by	
	19	Steamship *Francisca*, of Hull, landed 4, assisted to save vessel and	5
	Mar 12	Schooner *Intrepide*, of Gravelines, assisted to save vessel	

James Leath

1920	Feb 25	Smack *Emblem*, of Ramsgate, rendered assistance	
	Sep 2	Steamship *George Fisher*, of London, saved	7
	23	Steamship *Admiral Keyes*, of London, saved vessel and	7
	Dec 30	Barge *Hesper*, of Harwich, saved vessel and	4
1921	Oct 14	Motor vessel *Queen Philippa*, of London, stood by	
1922	Oct 2	Steam drifter *Elsay*, of Wick, stood by	
1923	Jan 11	Schooner *Fred*, of Simrishamn, assisted to save vessel	
1925	Nov 18	Steamship *Flashlight*, of London, rendered assistance	
1928	June 23	Schooner *Mary Ann*, of Guernsey, rendered assistance	

No.2 Station Boys

1867	Nov 25	Schooner *Assistant*, of Stavanger, stood by	
1869	Dec 0	Brig *Delegate*, of London, saved	
1870	Dec 31	Brig *Joseph and Thomas*, of South Shields, saved 10	
1871	Nov 14-5	Steamship *Benjamin Whitworth*, of Middlesborough, stood by	
	Dec 6	Barque *Typhon*, saved vessel	
	7	Brig *Aleza*, of Blyth (Shields), saved	2
1872	Mar 22	Brig *Ark*, of West Hartlepool, saved	6
	23	do., reboarded captain	
	Nov 15	Schooner *Mediateur*, of Nantes, assisted to save vessel and	6
	Dec 10	Brig *Pallion*, of Sunderland, assisted to save vessel	
		Brig *Lady Douglas*, of London, assisted to save vessel and 6	
1873	Nov 8	Schooner *Lord Howick*, of Maldon, saved vessel and	6
	16	Barque *Filatore*, of Genoa, saved	10
1874	Dec 9	Barque *Kingsdowne*, of South Shields, assisted to save vessel and	9
	20	Schooner *Victoria*, of Blyth, saved	5
		Brig *Sarah*, of Whitby, saved	6
1875	Jan 27	Brig *Pike*, of Shoreham, saved	7
	Mar 11	Schooner *Punch*, of Carnarvon, saved	6
	28	Brig *Thirteen*, of Sunderland, saved	8
	May 10	Cutter *Harkaway*, of Yarmouth, saved	6

The same lifeboat renamed *Godsend*

1875	Nov 16	Smack *Alice*, of Yarmouth, assisted to save vessel and	6
	21	Brig *Brodrenes Haab*, of Tonsberg, saved vessel and	6
1876	June 10	Ship *McNear*, of Boston (USA), landed 14 from light-vessel	
	Nov 4	Fishing smack *Phoebe*, of Yarmouth, saved	6
	Dec 23	Barque *Ingleborough*, of Hull, saved	13
1877	Jan 28	Brig *La Belle*, of Shoreham, saved 8 and some beachmen	
	Feb 27	Schooner *Sea Lark*, of Limerick, assisted to save vessel and	5
	Mar 9	Schooner *Harriet*, of Goole, assisted to save vessel	
	Nov 9	Barque *Augia*, of Guernsey, assisted to save vessel and	10
	12	Brig *Craigs*, of Whitby, assisted to save vessel	
		Brig *Lily*, of Guernsey, assisted to save vessel	
	Dec 12	Fishing smack *Martin Bayly*, of Yarmouth, saved vessel and	6
1878	Mar 28	Barque *Theresa*, of North Shields, landed	11
	Nov 9	Schooner *Milky Way*, of Fraserburgh, assisted to save vessel and	4
	Dec 19	Brig *Melita*, of Blyth, saved (including 10 beachmen)	16
1879	Jan 17	Brig *John*, of Hartlepool, stood by	
	28	Schooner *Hermann*, of Beriwck, landed 6 and stood by	
		do., (second service) assisted to save vessel	
	Feb 9	Steamship *Matin*, of Dundee, stood by	
	10	Dandy *William*, of London, saved (including 6 beachmen)	12
1880	Feb 15	Barque *Orion*, stood by	
1881	Jan 16	Barque *North Wales*, of London, saved	21
	Feb 2	Smack *Peace*, of Lowestoft, saved vessel and	5
	June 5	Barque *Alectro* of Malta, stood by	
	Oct 5	Fishing smack *Triton*, of Yarmouth, assisted to save vessel and	6
	Nov 16	Smack *Young Henry*, of Yarmouth, stood by	
	Oct 15	Brigantine *Menodora*, of Hartlepool, saved	6
	18	Brigantine *Fidele*, of Marstrand, assisted to save vessel and	6
1882	Mar 7	Barque *Canmore*, of Dundee, assisted to save vessel and	17
	Dec 1	Schooner *Brothers*, of Harwich, rendered assistance	
	17	Steamship *Bradley*, of Liverpool, assisted to save vessel and	15
1883	Jan 26	Brigantine *Dare*, of Sunderland, assisted to save vessel and	6
	Feb 14	Schooner *Don*, of Aberdeen, assisted to save vessel and	5
	Mar 1	Steamship *Barnsley*, of Grimsby, stood by	
	April 5	Brg *Spring*, of Guernsey, saved	9
	Sep 29	Schooner *Marguis of Aaglesea*, of Carnarvon, saved vessel and	4
1884	Dec 18	Dandy James *Garfield*, of Ipswich, assisted to save vessel and	4
1885	Jan 5	Dandy *Tyro*, of London, stood by	
	19	Brig *Triton*, of Svelvig, assisted to save vessel and	6
	June 19	Schooner *Agile*, of Goole, saved	4
	Sep 12	Dandy *Seabird*, of Yarmouth, saved vessel and	6
	Dec 28	Three-masted schooner *W.L.J.*, of Swansea, assisted to save vessel	
1886	Feb 25	Schooner *Julia*, of Lowestoft, saved vessel and	4
	Dec 10	Steamship *Watford*, of Sunderland, stood by	
1887	Sep 19	Fishing dandy *Vanguard*, of Great Yarmouth, saved vessel and	11
1888	Feb 4	Schooner *Shearwater*, of London, saved	5
	June 7	Fishing dandy *Ocean Star*, of Great Yarmouth, saved vessel and	6
	23	Ship *Tay*, of Glasgow, saved	27
	Oct 13-4	Schooner *Emperor*, of Banff, rendered assistance	

		Three-masted schooner *Girl of Devon*, of Plymouth, rendered assistance	
	Nov 1	Steamship *Ferndale*, of Sunderland, stood by	
	Dec 9	Fishing dandy *Cyprus*, of Great Yarmouth, stood by	
1889	Apr 14	teamship *Coleridge*, of Exeter, landed pilot	
	Aug 3	Three-masted schooner *Culzean Castle*, of Cork, rendered assistance	
		Brigantine *Aratus*, of Teignmouth, rendered assistance	
	Nov 30	Brigantine *Charles*, of Great Yarmouth, saved vessel and	6
1890	Jan 8	Brig *Primrose*, of Folkestone, stood by	
	June 16	Fishing dandy *Florence Mary*, of Great Yarmouth, saved vessel and	6
	Oct 29-30	Four-masted ship *Nile*, of Glasgow, rendered assistance	
1891	Oct 23	Schooner *C.S. Atkinson*, of Belfast, assisted to save vessel and	5
	31	Ketch barge *Brightlingsea*, of Harwich, saved	4
	Dec 8	Brig *Queen of the Isles*, of West Hartlepool, stood by	
	28	Schooner *Hannah Ransom*, of Southampton, saved vessel and	5

Beauchamp

1892	Jan 26	Fishing dandy *Canpida*, of Great Yarmouth, stood by	
	July 25	Ketch William and *Sarah Ann*, of Goole, saved vessel and	7
	Oct 7	Steamship *Idlewind*, of Sunderland, assisted to save vessel and	1
	Nov 11	A Scotch fishing boat, rendered assistance	
		A fishing dandy, of Lowestoft, stood by	
	13	Brig *Eugenie*, of Brevig, assisted to save vessel and	8
1893	Jan 23	Fishing dandy *Energy*, of Grimsby, saved	7
	24	Schooner *Cymbeline*, of London, stood by	
	May 31	Barque *Alexandria*, of Frederikstadt, assisted to save vessel	
	Oct 14	Schooner *W.D. Potts*, of Carnarvon, assisted to save vessel and	6
1894	Jan 6	Barque *Wallace J. John*, of Gluckstadt, landed 12 from Cockle light-vessel	
	Feb 11	Steamship *Resolven*, of Cardiff, transferred 35 labourers to a tug and stood by	
	Apr 19	Barquentine *Clachnacuddin*, of Guernsey, saved	8
	May 27	Ketch *Waterlily*, of Goole, assisted to save vessel and	
	July 24	Brigantine *Navigator*, of Lowestoft, saved vessel and	5
1896	Nov 8	Ship *Soudan*, of Liverpool, saved	8
1897	Feb 21-2	Steamship *Varna*, of London, stood by	
	Apr 28	Brigantine *Watch*, of Hull, stood by	
	June 4-6	Steamship *Laleham*, of Newcastle, assisted to save vessel	
	Nov 28	Barge *Lord Wolseley*, of London, landed 1 from Cockle light-vessel	
1898	Jan 16	Schooner *Thomas*, of Lowestoft, stood by and rendered assistance	
		Ketch *Blue Jacket*, of Wells, stood by	
	Feb 25	Schooner *Hermann*, of Boekzetelerfehn, saved	5
1899	Feb 14	Steamship *Russian Prince*, of Newcastle, rendered assistance	
	July 4	Ketch *Via*, of Ramsgate, assisted to save vessel	
	Sep 16	Dandy William, of Great Yarmouth, saved	10
	23	Schooner *Parthenia*, of Great Yarmouth, assisted to save vessel and	6
	30	Lugger *Alica*, of Great Yarmouth, saved lugger and	3
	Oct 9	Steamship *Achilles*, of South Shields, stood by	
	Nov 8	Lugger *Palestine*, of Banff, saved	8
1900	Jan 18	Ketch *Temperance Pledge*, of Scarborough, saved vessel and	2
	Oct 13	Dandy *Corsair*, of Calais, stood by	
	Nov 24	Schooner *St Austell*, of Fowey, saved abandoned vessel	
	26	Brigantine *Northern Star*, of South Shields, rendered assistance	
1901	Oct 10	Dandy *Orient*, of Lowestoft, assisted to save vessel and	9

Nancy Lucy

1903	July 18	Steamship *Bramiam*, of London, rendered assistance	
	Oct 24	Steam drifter *Shamrock*, of Peterhead, assisted to save vessel	
1905	Jun 29-30	Ketch *Amelia Ann*, of Goole, rendered assistance	
	July 31	Fishing smack *Fawn*, of Yarmouth, stood by	
	Oct 19	Brigantine *Primula*, of Istorp, saved	8
1906	Aug 4	Smack *Gladys*, of Lowestoft. stood by	
	Sep 18	Barque *Anna Precht*, of Mariehamn, landed 1 and saved	6
	Oct 17	Fishing boat *Nazzurullah*, of St Monance, stood by	
		A tug, stood by	
1907	July 6	Ketch *Charlotte Kilner*, of Goole, stood by	
	Sep 11	Schooner *Zwaantje Cornelia*, of Groningen, stood by	
	Dec 18	Steamship *Andalusia*, of London, stood by	
1909	Aug 8	Steamship *Tarnholm*, of Copenhagen, stood by	
1910	Aug 31	Schooner *William and Alice*, of Hull, stood by	
1914	Oct 1	Steamship *Haller*, of Hull, assisted to save vessel	
1917	July 8	Steamship *City of Oxford*, of Hull, assisted to save vessel and	130
1918	Nov 4	Steamship *Juno*, of Hull, stood by	
1919	Sep 18-9	Steamship *Incholm*, of Leith, stood by	
	Nov 28-9	Steam drifter *Emily Reach*, of Buckie, stood by	
	30	Lighter *Beaujolais*, of Havre, rendered assistance	
1926	July 9	Steam trawler *Vigilant*, of Hull, rendered assistance	
	Aug 9	Motor trawler *Qualia*, of Lowestoft, stood by	

Charles Burton

1930	Aug 16	Steam trawler *Jean Dore*, of Boulogne, stood by	
1931	June 17	Fishing smack *Samaritan*, of Lowestoft, stood by	
1934	May 21	Cutter yacht *Gariad*, of Cardiff, stood by	
	Aug 7	Fishing boat *Handy Billy*, of Yarmouth, saved	2
1935	Jan 11	Steam trawler *Prosper*, of Ostend, rendered assistance	
	Oct 2	Motor boat *Beaty*, of Yarmouth, stood by	
	Nov 25	Steam drifter *Ocean Sprite*, of Yarmouth, rendered assistance	
	Dec 7	Steam drifter *Young Sam*, of Yarmouth, stood by	
1936	Apr 25	Auxiliary cutter yacht *Mavan*, of Southampton, stood by	
		do., saved yacht and	2
1937	Jan 1-2	Steamship *Crackshot*, of Newcastle, rendered assistance and stood by	
	3	Sailing boat *Sea Bird*, of Caister, saved boat and	7
	Nov 25	Steam drifter *Corn Rig*, of Buckie, stood by	
1939	July 10	Yacht *Sarah Ann*, of Maldon, rendered assistance	
1940	Apr 15	Motor fishing boat *Don't Know*, of Great Yarmouth, saved boat and 2	
	May 25	HM Trawler *Charles Boyes*, saved	2

Jose Neville

1943	June 25	USAF Flying Fortress aircraft, salved wreckage	
	26	British aircraft, gave help	
1944	Jan 6	LC(M).1144 and LC(M).1229, escorted craft	

	Aug 28	Bather, saved	1
1945	Apr 22	Steamship *Wilno*, of Gdynia, escorted	
	Sep 27	Steamship *Brightside*, of Middlesborough, gave help	
1946	Feb 26	Motor vessel *Caribia*, of Delfzijl, saved	8
1947	Jan 11	Steamship *Ewell*, of London, gave help (two launches)	
	12	do., (third launch), gave help	
	Oct 12	Motor vessel *Cyprian Coast*, of Newcastle, stood by	
1948	May 2	Sealing skiff *Boy Ray*, of Great Yarmouth, saved skiff and	4
	June 15	Steam tanker *Thule*, of London, gave help	
	Sep 11	Motor yacht *Switha*, of Inverness, gave help	
1949	April 2	Motor vessel *David M*, of London, gave help	
	3	Motor fishing boat *Beatty*, of Great Yarmouth, gave help	
1950	July 8	Motor yacht *Starshine*, gave help	
	Nov 22	Motor vessel *Traquair*, of Leith, gave help	
1951	Mar 17	Steamship *Southport*, of Glasgow, gave help	
	May 6	Motor barge *Glenway*, of Rochester, stood by	
	June 17	Yacht *Idler*, of Great Yarmouth, gave help	
	Aug 9	Motor yacht *Dimcyl*, of Lowestoft, saved yacht and	6
	21	Fishing boat *Cornucopia*, of Lossiemouth, gave help	
	Dec 28	Motor barge *Olive May*, of London, gave help	
1952	Feb 29	Motor vessel *Serenity*, of London, gave help	
	May 2	Steamship *Craig*, of Leith, stood by	
		do., gave help	
	Dec 3	Fast Patrol Boat *Havoernen*, of Royal Danish Navy, saved	9
	5	do., gave help	
		do., gave help	
	26	Tugs *Aegir* and *Garm*, of Denmark, landed 2 sick men	
1953	Jan 8	Motor vessel *Maraat*, of Rotterdam, gave help	
1954	June 15	HM Motor Launch No.323, gave help	
1955	Jan 12	Motor vessel *Nissan*, of Halmstad (Sweden), gave help	
	Feb 13	Motor trawler *St Pierre-Eglise*, of Boulogne, stood by vessel	
	14	do., gave help	
	16	do., gave help	
	Mar 11	Motor tug *Alcha*, of Southend, gave help	
	May 30	Steamship *Harfry*, of London, gave help	
	June 12	Shrimpboat *Try*, of Great Yarmouth, escorted vessel	
	Aug 7	Yacht *Jemima Puddleduck*, of Hull, saved	3
	15	Steamship *Keynes*, of London, landed a sick amn	
	Sep 2	Dinghy, of Caister, saved boat and	3
	Dec 12	Steam trawler *Thracian*, of Grimsby, saved	6
1956	April 2	Cross Sand Light-vessel, landed an injured man	
	Oct 12	Fishing boat *Golden Gift*, of Great Yarmouth, gave help	
1957	July 22	Motor vessel *Fiducia*, of Holland, gave help	
	29	Fishing boat *Valerie* and houseboat *Miranda*, gave help	
1958	Jan 26	Motor vessel *Fosdyke Trader*, of Hull, gave help	
	May 11	Small boat, saved boat and	2
	30	Motor vessel *Lijnbaan*, of Rotterdam, gave help	
	Aug 16	Motor boat *Ocean Queen*, saved boat and	2
1959	Jan 15	Steamship *John Charrington*, of London, stood by vessel	
	May 17	Fishing boat *Eileen Summer*, escorted vessel	
	July 9	Fishing boat *Sea Hawk*, of London, escorted boat	
	Oct 9	Fishing boat *Happy Spring*, of Great Yarmouth, saved boat and	3
1960	Oct 19	Motor vessel *Harry Richardson*, gave help	

	Dec 4	Fishing vessel *Gloamin N*, saved boat and	3
	13	Barge *Will Everard*, gave help	
		Motor vessel *Serenity*, gave help	
1961	Feb 24	Steamship *Gudveig*, of Oslo, gave help	
1962	Apr 21	Tug *Danny*, of Aberdeen, saved vessel and	7
1963	Jan 17	Motor vessel *Maria W*, of Rotterdam, gave help and escorted tug	
	25	Motor vessel *Crescence*, of Rochester, gave help	
	27	Motor vessel *Crescence*, of Rochester, gave help	
	April 8	Trawler *Kirkley*, of Lowestoft, recovered liferaft and saved	8
	Aug 22	Trawler *Ixous*, of Ostende, gave help	
	Oct 16	Fishing vessel *Endeavour III*, of Harwich, saved boat and	2
	Dec 15	Trawler *Loch Lorgan*, saved	7

The Royal Thames

1964	Aug 16	Cabin cruiser *Redcap*, saved boat and	5
	22	Motor cruiser *Cairnbin*, saved boat and	2
	Oct 11	Motor vessel *Elation*, of Rochester, gave help	
	Nov 20	Trawler *Ada Kerby*, of Lowestoft, gave help	
1965	Oct 29	Fishing boat *Catherine Ann*, of Great Yarmouth, saved boat and	3
1966	Feb 12	Trawler *Ira*, of Lowestoft, stood by vessel	
	May 6	Aircraft, recovered wreckage	
	June 23	Motor vessel *Regency*, of London, stood by vessel	
1967	June 22	RAF Helicopter, landed body and recovered wreckage	
	Oct 9	Fishing vessel *Girl Pat*, of Great Yarmouth, gave help	
		Fishing boat *Oliver*, gave help	
	Nov 1	Fishing boats *Sailor Prince* and *Joan and Doris*, escorted boats	
1968	July 22	Trawler Catherine *Shaun*, of Fleetwood, landed an injured man	
	Sep 2	Yacht *Midge*, gave help	
	30	Fishing boat *Beatty* gave help	
1969	May 2	Motor fishing vessel *Kaster*, of Lowestoft, recovered wreckage	
	July 12	Speed-boat *Miss Britannia*, saved boat	
	Aug 11	Motor fishing vessel *Winaway*, saved boat and	4

Volunteer Rescue Service – Small rescue boats

1970	Mar 15	Motor vessel *Interwave*, of Groningen (Holland), gave help	
	July 21	Sailing dinghy, gave help	
1971	July 15	Sailing dinghy, saved dinghy and	1
	Aug 8	Motor vessel *Galway Blazer*, gave help	
	7	Swimmer, landed	1
	Nov 1	Tanker Jacquilene *Broere*, of Dordrecht (Holland), gave help	
1972	July 10	Sailing dinghy, gave help	
	Aug 9	Speedboat in tow of fishing boat, gave help	
	17	Rubber dinghy, saved dinghy and	2
	Nov 1	Motor fishing boat *Joan and Doris*, stood by	
	22	Fishing boat, gave help	
1973	Mar 22	Ship's boat, gave help	
	May 28-9	Motor fishing vessel *Glint*, of Flekkefjord (Norway), gave help	
	June 13	Catamaran *Sis*, of Stockton, gave help	
	July 29	Motor cruiser *Which Way*, gave help	

Aug 7   Speedboat *Evening Cloud*, gave help
    14   Motor boat *Seabird*, gave help
          Swimmer, gave help
    29   Rubber dinghy, gave help
Dec 12   Rowing boat, gave help

Shirley Jean Adye

1973	Aug 17	Motor boat *Joan And Doris*, of Great Yarmouth, gave help	
	Sep 23	Trimaran *Trifid*, saved boat and	2
	Oct 25	Motor yacht *White Heather*, gave help	
	26	Motor fishing vessel *Lead Us*, of Great Yarmouth, gave help	
	Dec 2	Motor vessel *See Penmar*, of Germany, stood by vessel	
1974	June 10	Motor cruiser *Gipsy*, assisted to save vessel	
	Nov 13	Motor yacht *Et Tu*, saved boat and	2
1975	Jan 5	Motor vessel *Lady Sheena*, of Rochester, saved vessel and	4
	July 6	Motor cruiser *Nymrod*, of Great Yarmouth, assisted to save vessel	
	Aug 2	Motor cruiser *Eastern Promise*, gave help	
	2-3	Motor vessel *Kai*, of Singapore, assisted vessel	
	5	Tug *Sun 26*, stood by vessel	
	12	Yacht *Cascara*, of Holland, assisted vessel	
		Motor cruiser *Dilly*, saved boat and	2
	Dec 1	Motor vessel *Proton*, of Holland, escorted vessel	
	12	Motor vessel *Alexandria*, of Egypt, gave help	
1976	Feb 22	Fishing vessel *Wydale*, gave help	
	Mar 25	Shetland sailboard, saved board and	1
	Oct 20	Motor fishing vessel *Sylvia*, gave help	
	Nov 5	Motor barge *Kate*, saved vessel and	2
1977	Apr 8	Motor vessel *Baltic*, of Denmark, stood by vessel	
	18	Motor vessel *Star River*, of Faroes, assisted to save vessel and	5
	July 19	Catamaran *Katachuck*, gave help	
	28	Motor vessel *Cape Shore*, gave help	
	Sep 1	Yacht *Zulu Maid*, gave help	
	24	Motor fishing vessel *Eve*, of Wisbech, escorted and assisted boat	
1978	Jan 12	Motor vessel *Sea Diamond*, of Greece, recovered and landed a body	
	July 3	Dredger *Hoveringham VI*, stood by vessel	
	Oct 25	Trawler *Granada*, of Lowestoft, gave help	
	26	Landing craft *Kermit*, gave help	
1979	Dec 4	Trawler *Suffolk Chieftain*, of Lowestoft, saved	11
		5 do., assisted to refloat vessel	
1980	Aug 20	Motor cruiser *Misty Morn*, gave help	
	Oct 3	Motor vessel *Aaron Firth*, of Ramsey, gave help	
	11	Brigantine *Luna*, of Holland, stood by vessel	
1981	Apr 27	Motor cruiser *Bronco*, escorted vessel	
	June 20	Motor yacht *La Concha Dos*, gave help	
	July 27	Training ship *Sir Winston Churchill*, stood by and assisted vessel	
1982	April 1	Rig stand-by trawler *Scamption*, stood by vessel	
1983	Mar 13	Rig stand-by trawler *St David's*, stood by vessel	
1984	April 5	Rig standby trawler *Anguilla*, gave help	
	28	Motor fishing vessel *Tidemaster*, gave help	
	June 12	Yacht *Oedieg*, of Germany, gave help	

	24	Yacht *Auldgirth*, saved	2
	Sep 9	Sailboard, landed 1 from ILB	
	18	Motor fishing vessel *Joan Linda* [IN.26], gave help	
	Oct 19	Whelk boat *Pamasuki* [MN.149], gave help	
	Dec	9-10 Motor fishing boat *Avocet* [CO.363], gave help	
1985	Jan 11-2	Motor fishing boat *Sharon* [JH.50], gave help	
	June 3-4	Motor vessel *Star Viking*, of Faroes, stood by vessel	
	Aug 11	Motor fishing boat *Ann Christine*, saved boat and	10
1986	Aug 4-5	Dredger *Arco Tees*, assisted to save vessel	
	Sep 22	Motor fishing boat *Sue Ii*, gave help	
	Nov 18	Rig supply vessel *Seaforth Conqueror*, saved	8
	19	do., gave help	
1987	Apr 2	Motor launch *Akelda*, of Guernsey, assisted to save vessel	
1988	May 29	Yacht *G-Whizz*, gave help	
	Aug 3	Fishing vessel *Nicola Dawn* [YH.154], gave help	
1989	Jan 2	Motor fishing boat *Spray* [YH.102], gave help	
	22	Cabin cruiser *Jan May*, gave help	
	June 30	Cabin cruiser *Sampurna*, saved boat and	3
	July 1	Motor vessel *Collet* [LT.107], gave help	
	18	Motor yacht *Resolution*, saved boat and	5
	30	Yacht *Secret & Perquita*, escorted vessel	
	Nov 1	Fishing boat *Comet* [YH.238], escorted boat	
1990	May 3	Motor fishing vessel *Beryl Ann* [LT.14], gave help	
	25	Motor fishing vessel *Ann Isabella* [LO.61], gave help	
	Sep 9	Yacht *Contessa*, gave help	

Bernard Matthews

1991	July 18	Motor trawler *David John* [A.991], stood by vessel	
	Aug 20	Fishing vessel *Sophie Dawn* [LT.22], gave help	
	25	Fishing vessel *Cheryl M* [YH.49], assisted to save vessel and landed 2 from ILB	
	Oct 10	Motor fishing vessel *Orion* [LT.15], saved vessel and	2
	23	Catamaran *Rainbow Runner*, of Wells, saved vessel and	1
1992	June 6	Motor cruiser *Macdog*, of Southampton, gave help	
	19	Yacht *Sea Moon*, saved yacht and	2
	July 20-1	Yacht *Cherokee* II, saved yacht, two dogs and	2
		Yacht *Ajaia*, gave help	
	23	Motor yacht *Ahh Bee*, gave help	
	Aug 2	Dinghy, saved dinghy and	3
	9	Motor vessel *Hoo Creek*, of London, gave help	
	16	Catamaran *Knock Out*, saved	2
	27	Fishing vessel *Nicola Dawn*, gave help	
	29	Yacht *Alderia*, of Holland, stood by vessel	
	Sep 17	Motor vessel *Selina*, of Honduras, assisted to save vessel	
	Dec 12	Motor fishing vessel *Toriki* [LN.17], saved vessel and	2
1993	May 11-2	Motor vessel *Sooneck*, of Germany, assisted to save vessel	
	July 14	Helicopter, stood by	
	Aug 15	Fishing vessel *Sea Ranger*, of Great Yarmouth, gave help	
		Diving boat *Rough Diamond*, saved boat and	5
	16-7	Training ship *Martin*, saved vessel and	7
	Sep 16	Yacht *Donna Clair*, escorted vessel	

	Oct 27	Motor cruiser *Meridian*, of Rye, saved boat and	3
	Dec 9	Fishing vessel *Vroun Grietje*, searched for missing man in extreme conditions
1994	Apr 9	Crane barge DB.101, of Holland, landed three injured men
	18	Crane barge DB.101, of Holland, assisted to save barge
	27	Motor fishing vessel *Ever Hopeful*, gave help
	May 21	Yacht *Intrepid*, saved yacht and	2
	June 12	Motor fishing vessel *Ever Hopeful*, escorted vessel
	17-8	Motor fishing vessel *Catherina Annie* [LT.45], gave help
	19-20	Sail Training Ship *James Cook*, gave help
	28	Steam yacht *Corola*, saved yacht
	July 31	Motor fishing vessel *Annebella* [LT.308], gave help
	Aug 1	Dving boat *Cormorant*, gave help
	9	Motor yacht *Smokey Bandit*, saved vessel, two dogs and	4
	27	Motor yacht *Big Easy*, saved yacht and	3
	Sep 19	Fishing boat *Ruth* [YH.269], gave help
	Oct 10	Motor fishing vessel *Nicola Dawn*, gave help
1995	Jan 11-2	Motor vessel *Ven Dome*, of Gibralter, assisted vessel
	Mar 22	Fishing vessel *Breydon Warrior*, of Yarmouth, saved vessel and	2
	Mar 28	Motor cruiser *Captain Simon*, gave help
	Apr 6	Fishing boat *Denise Yh168*, gave help
	May 28-9	Flares reported, no recorded service
	30	Motor fishing boat *Elizabeth Ann*, gave help
	June 12	Yacht *Bullfrog*, saved yacht (and a cat) and	1
	21	Motor fishing vessel *Seagull LN22*, gave help
	July 4-5	Motor fishing vessel *Alber GY194*, saved vessel and	1
	5-6	Motor cruiser *Gemma Louise*, towed to Yarmouth, gave help
	10	Trimaran *Dragonfly*, saved vessel and	3
	18-9	Tug *Baltagi IV*, of Beirut, aground on Scroby, gave help
	30	Recovered Zodiac Dinghy, assisted to help sick person
	Aug 1-2	Yacht *Quartet*, gave help
	11-2	Motor barge *Berian*, of Holland, gave help
	23	Mystery call for assistance, no service
	30-1	Search for missing divers, no service
	Sep 9	Yacht *Francipani*, of Brixham, saved yacht and	2
	24	Yacht *Madame*, of Holland, saved yacht and	9
	Oct 1	Yacht *Sequina*, wrecked on Scroby, saved	4
	13	Motor yacht *Joy*, gave help
	Dec 15-6	Helicopter assisting rock barge, stood by
1996	Apr 5	Motor fishing vessel *Girl Jane* SD80, gave help
	June 27	Yacht *Sweet Thursday*, gave help
	28	Yacht *Emma B*, gave help
	July 8	Motor cruiser *Perfect Lady*, gave help
	22	Yacht *Sweet Sensation*, gave help
	Aug 1-2	Ex-Fishing vessel *Summer Rose*, saved vessel and	1
	8	Motor cruiser *Sea Hanser*, saved boat and	2
	Oct 9	Fishing vessel *Swy-Y-Mor* BS68, saved vessel and	2
	30	Tug *Zwerver 1*, of Holland, escorted tug
	Nov 10	Fishing boat *Tom Kat*, landed a body and stood by
	11	Capsized tug *Bever*, of Holland, stood by tug and recovered liferaft
	Dec 16	Motor fishing vessel *Brejon*, gave help
		Motor fishing vessel TH61, gave help
1997	Mar 28	Motor cruiser *Sweet Heart*, gave help

	Apr 4	Motor yacht *Anna Matilda*, of Poole, escorted yacht	
	July 16	Search for missing bot, no service recorded	
	Aug 3	Motor yacht *Orinoco*, escorted yacht	
		Missing divers boat, no service recorded	
	13	Search for missing divers, no service recorded	
	30-1	Red flares reported, no servicce recorded	
	Oct 25	Motor boat *Talefin*, gave help	
	Nov 9-10	Search for missing woman, no service recorded	
1998	Jan 26	Recovered floating hazard	
	June 20	Searched for missing diver	
	11	Yacht *Paper Lady*, saved yacht and	2
	19	Dutch barge *Vrouwe Cornelia*, gave help	
	Aug 3	Yacht *Josie Ross*, saved yacht and	3
	12	Yacht *Innis*, gave help	
	Sep 4	Motor boat *Highlight* YH 563, escorted boat	
	26	Diving boat *Crusader*, gave help	
1999	May 16	Yacht *Lydia May*, saved yacht and	1
	July 16	Search for missing man, no recorded service	
	Aug 23	Motor cruiser *Titan Lady*, gave help	
	Sep 25	Motor fishing boat *Willing Boy*, gave help	
	Oct 12	Naval tender *Prada*, gave help	
	18	acht Barracuda, saved yacht and	6
	Dec 1	Red flares, no recorded service	
2000	Mar 6	Missing angler, gave help	
	Apr 22	Yacht *Swinstar II*, gave help	
	May 23	Yacht *Okapi*, gave help	
	27	Yacht *Zippa*, saved vessel and	3
	July 1	Yacht *Fermata*, recovered capsized yacht	
	2	Motor cruiser *Jenny*, gave help	
	10	Sailing smack *Excelsior*, assisted to save vessel and	9
	31	Fishing vessel *Reliant*, gave help	
	Oct 28-9	Yacht *Haggard*, escorted vessel	
	Nov 25	Yacht *Cavertine*, saved yacht and	1

Jim Davidson Inshore Lifeboat

1995	May 28	Injured man on board Gorleston ILB, assisted to land	
	July 14	Windwurfer in trouble, no service	
	Aug 12	Mising persons, no service	
	21	Rubber dinghy, saved	3
	Oct 1	Yacht *Sequina*, recovered equipment	
	26	Search for reported dead body, no service	
1996	June 27	Yacht *Sweet Thursday*, gave help	
	Nov 11	Capsized tug *Bever*, of Holland, assisted naval divers	
1997	Apr 13	Outboard motor dinghy, escorted to shore	
	July 13	Woman in the sea, saved	1
	Aug 3	Missing divers boat, no service recorded	
	14	Drifting dinghy, no service recorded	
	15	Dinghy in trouble, no service recorded	
	19	Yacht Free and easy, landed a sick man	
	Oct 26	Man in the sea, no service recorded	
1998	June 7	Dinghy, saved dinghy and	2

	Aug 6	Boy on airbed, saved	1
	12	Dinghy, escorted	
		Dinghy, gave help	
	14	Dinghy, stood by	
	17	Dinghy, saved dinghy and	2
		Dinghy, saved dinghy and	2
	20	Two girls on rubber rings, saved	2
	Oct 22	Fishing boat *Boy Clive*, gave help	
1999	June 20	Two dinghies, saved dinghies and	2
	July 16	Two dinghies, escorted	
	16	Search for missing man, no recorded service	
	Aug 2	Two swimmers in trouble, no recorded service	
	18	Three dinghies, escorted	
2000	May 12	Overturned boat, recovered boat	
	June 12	Dinghy, escorted	
		Dinghy, saved dinghy and	2
	July 28	Dinghy, saved dinghy and	2
		29 Fishing boat *Meteor*, gave help	
	Aug 12	Dinghy, escorted dinghy	
	15	Person in water, gave help	

Appendix 3
Personnel summary

Honorary Secretary

Matthew Butcher	1859-70
Revd G.W. Steward, MA	1868-78
Revd E.G.H. Murrell	1878-89
A. Frank Clowes	1896-1908
William Case, MRCS	1900-10
H.W. Youell	1910-14
Edward Boning	1914-35
A.J. Main	1935-46
M.C. McAvoy	1946-69

Retired when station closed by RNLI in 1969

Coxswain

Ben Hodds	1845-72
Phillip George	1872-87
James Haylett jnr	1887-1900
Aaron Haylett	1900-1901
John 'Whampo' Brown	1902-03
John 'Spratt' Haylett	1903-19
Charles Lacock	1919-35
Joseph Woodhouse	1935-50
James Brown	1950-56
John Albert Plummer	1956-69
Alfred Edmund Brown	1973-81
Benny Read	1981-91
Richard Thurlow	1991-

Second Coxswain

James Henry Haylett, snr	?
William Brown	?-1901
John Plummer	?
Charles Lacock	1917-18
Walter Haylett	1918-29
James H. Brown	1948-50
Alfred Edmund Brown	1950-69

Joe Woodhouse, father of Skipper Woodhouse, an ex-herring drifter skipper and Coxswain until 1950, seen in 1934/35 in front of the old white shed on the beach. The collecting box now stands in Caister cemetery close to the Beauchamp memorial. (Caister Lifeboat House)

Appendix 4
Bibliography

Anonymous: *The Caister Lifeboats* (1972).

Cannell, John: *The men who never turned back* (2000).

Farr, Grahame: *Papers on Life-boat History, No.2: George Palmer's lifeboats 1828-47, with Allied Types and Variants* (1975).

Higgins, David: *The Beachmen* (Terence Dalton, Lavenham, Suffolk, 1987).

Leach, Nicholas: *The Origins of the lifeboat Service* (1992).

Long, Neville: *Lights of East Anglia* (Terence Dalton, Lavenham, Suffolk, 1983).

Malster, Robert: *Saved from the Sea: The story of life-saving services on the East Anglian coast* (Terence Dalton, Lavenham, Suffolk, 1974).

Morris, Jeff: *The Story of the Great Yarmouth & Gorleston Lifeboats* (1997).

Tooke, Colin: *Caister – Beachboats and Beachmen* (Poppyland Publishing, North Walsham, Norfolk, nd).

Wiltshire, Roger: *Norfolk's Lifeboats: A Portrait in Photographs and Picture Postcards* (S B Publications, Seaford, Sussex, 1994).